Contents

Preface	v
Holding Tools	2
Measuring Tools	3
Marking Tools	4
Cutting Aids	8
Saws	9
Planes	15
Chisels	25
Boring Tools	28
Driving Tools	32
Shaping Tools	36
Maintenance	40
Machine Tools	47
Portable Electrical Tools	54

Craft and Design in Wood

1 Materials, Constructions and Finishes

2 Hand and Machine Tools

3 Design and Allied Craft Techniques

1 Materials, Constructions and Finishes

The author presents a detailed and attractive account of wood, manufactured boards and associated plastics. He deals with all basic joints and constructions and includes knock-down fittings and assembly techniques. The use of traditional and modern plastic finishes is fully explained. Book 1 concludes with an excellent hardware section.

3 Design and Allied Craft Techniques

Traditional drawing methods are thoroughly described in the early sections. The account of sketching and room planning is succeeded by three examples of approach to product design.

Sections on veneering, upholstery, carving, turning, and laminating serve as an introductory sample of some of the subsidiary crafts covered by the examination syllabus.

Pupils will find the last section an invaluable guide in preparation for these examinations which include a study or project as part of course work.

The Craft and Design Scheme

The main feature of all three books in this series is that the basic text is linked to a vast number of photographs and simple line drawings. This combination of notes and illustrations is ideal for fourth and fifth form pupils of all abilities. The author has successfully shown how modern materials and methods have replaced some traditional techniques.

This Book
2 Hand and Machine Tools

The author describes hand tools in separate sections according to their function. These sections include marking, measuring and testing tools; saws; planes; chisels; boring, driving and shaping tools.

He illustrates basic maintenance techniques simply but fully. In the machine tool section, the author emphasises safety precautions. His description of portable electric tools covers the requirements of most examining board syllabuses.

Craft and Design in Wood

2 Hand and Machine Tools

David M. Willacy

HUTCHINSON EDUCATIONAL LTD
3 Fitzroy Square, London W1

London Melbourne Sydney Auckland
Wellington Johannesburg Cape Town
and agencies throughout the world

First published 1974
© David M. Willacy 1974

Printed in Great Britain on smooth wove paper
by Anchor Press, and bound by Wm. Brendon,
both of Tiptree, Essex.

ISBN 0 09 114721 2

To Susan Laura

The Bench
Holding Tools

The Bench

The common woodworking bench has a thick working top, bench stops, and a vice fitted at each side. Cupboards for tool and work storage are below.

The bench illustrated is more adaptable. The top is made of well-seasoned beech, supported by an underframe which is bolted to the floor. A storage box is attached to either side or the end of the bench.
The front vice enables wide pieces of wood to be held vertically. The illustration shows comb corner joints being fitted.

The tail vice will hold wood horizontally. Pairs of slots are mortised along the length of the bench-top. Metal dogs fit into these and into the tail vice.
Use for holding wood for planing, rebating, mortising and for cramping light work.

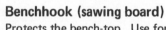

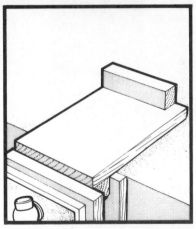

Holdfast

Fits through a metal collar recessed into the traditional bench-top. Remove when not in use.
Use to hold boards being grooved or rebated.

Benchhook (sawing board)

Protects the bench-top. Use for holding small sections of wood being sawn across the grain.

Shooting board

Use for trimming the ends of legs and boards. Use a try-plane for large work and a block plane for small sections. A side-handled technical jack plane is available (see page 16).

Tool storage

The rack illustrated is attached to the underframe of the bench shown above.

Holding Tools
Mitre cutter and Cramp

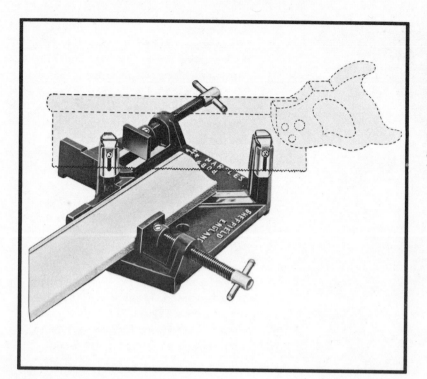

The mitre joint, generally cut at an angle of 45° is commonly used on the corners of picture frames. The joint can be sawn on a wood mitre block or in a mitre box and trimmed on a mitre shooting board. Alternatively, hold the wood firmly in a metal cramp and use a backsaw, slotted between metal guides to ensure a clean and accurate joint.

The cutter can also be used as a mitre cramp.

Mitre cramp

Frame Cramp

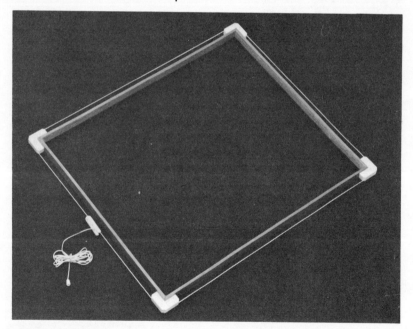

The Stanley frame cramp is used to hold mitred frames that are only being glued and not pinned.

The polypropylene corner jaws are strong and will not stick to surplus glue.

The terylene cord will not fray or break in normal use and is secured by a non-slip cleat. Can be used effectively on frames with side lengths from 100 to 750mm.

Web Cramp

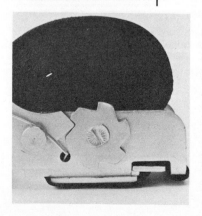

The Stanley web cramp is for heavy-duty cramping of large or awkward shaped items. The nylon webbing (nearly 4 metres long) will not damage a finished surface. Use for boat building, square frames and laminating.

The simple ratchet on which the web is tightened is operated by a screwdriver or a spanner.

Measuring Tools
Steel Rule

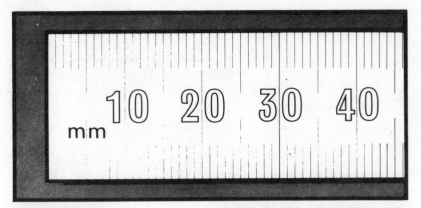

Steel rules are machined and marked for use when measurements must be accurate.
300 mm rule for bench use.
150 mm rule for carrying in the pocket.
The smallest divisions are millimetres which are subdivided by longer lines into units of 5 and 10 mm (one centimetre).

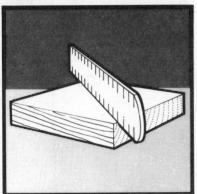

The zero end enables gauge setting and measuring from corners to be done accurately.

The edges are ground parallel to each other. Use as a straight edge for testing small surfaces for flatness.

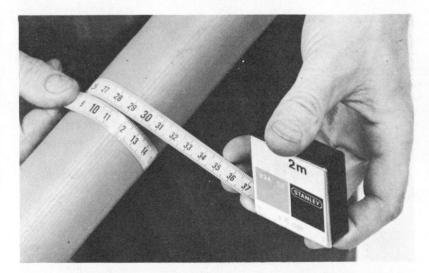

Pocket rule blades are made of thin flexible steel. The best have a crackproof finish and when released retract into the case.
The case label indicates the blade length (usually 2m or 3m) and the width of the case itself.
This information is needed when an internal measurement is being taken, for example,

distance indicated on tape   418mm
width of case   50mm
total inside measurement   468mm

Use for measurements over 300mm, table diameters and marking out boards.

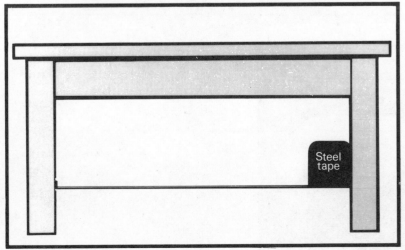

Marking Tools
Pencils

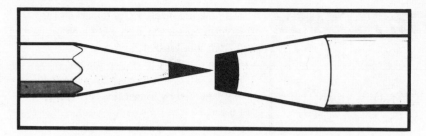

Use a round-leaded sharp pencil for marking out details of joints.

Use a square-leaded carpenter's pencil, which will not break easily, for marking out boards.

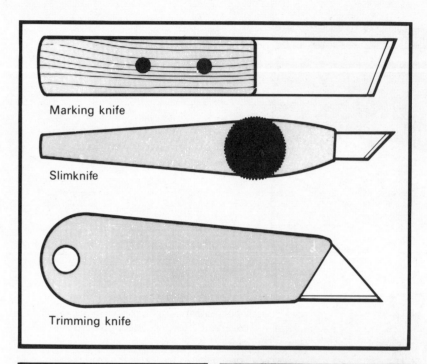

Marking knife

Slimknife

Trimming knife

The traditional marking knife has a steel blade riveted to a hardwood handle. It is sharpened on one side only.

The Stanley Slimknife has interchangeable narrow blades.

The Stanley trimming knife can also be fitted with various blades. It is strong and versatile.

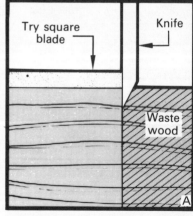

Try square blade

Knife

Waste wood

A

B

Uses
A. The traditional knife being used to mark a shoulder line. Used with a try-square the knife cuts a square shoulder to saw against.

B. The position of dovetail sockets being marked from tails with a 'Slimknife'

C. Alternative blades for use in the trimming knife. 5193 — for scoring or slicing round intricate shapes.

D. 5194 — for scoring, cutting and deburring the edge of decorative plastic laminates.

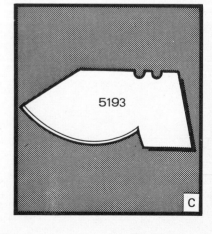

5193

C

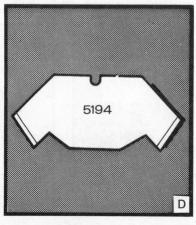

5194

D

Try-square

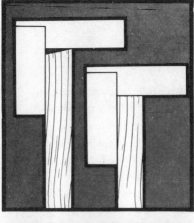

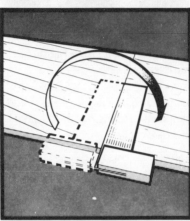

The steel blade of a try-square is securely riveted to either a wood handle with a brass face or an ABS plastic handle which has an accurately machined face.
Use to test the squareness of board edges.

Use as a guide for accurate vertical drilling.

Use (with a knife) for marking shoulder lines which are to be sawn.

Test for accuracy by setting the handle against a true edge and marking a line. Reverse the square and check alignment.

Mitre Square

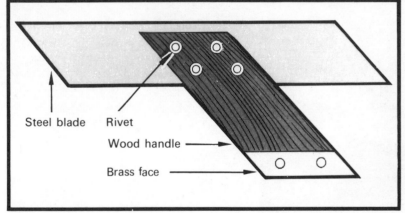

Steel blade   Rivet

Wood handle →

Brass face →

The steel blade is set into the wood handle at an angle of 45°. Use for marking out and/or testing a set angle of 45°, for example, mitred shoulders.
Note: Use a mitre cutter when cutting picture frame joints (see page 2).

Sliding Bevel

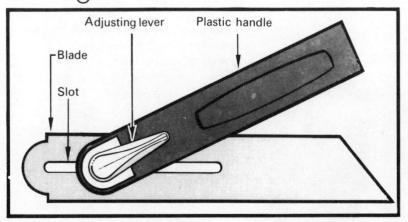

Adjusting lever   Plastic handle

Blade

Slot

The steel blade is slotted into a wood, metal or plastic handle.
A simple lever releases and sets the blade at the angle required. Use for marking dovetails and tapers on table legs.

Templates Paper/Card

Templates are full size patterns which enable work to be set out quickly and accurately.

Use a paper template, which is often cut from a full-size working drawing, when a shape is to be drawn only once.

A template to be used more often is cut from card.

Hardboard and Plywood

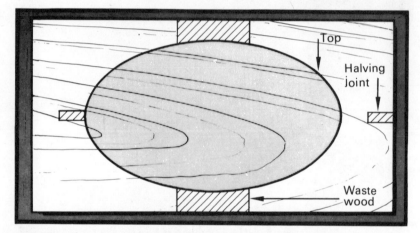

Top

Halving joint

Waste wood

Large templates are made from hardboard or plywood.

The templates are easily labelled and stored. Note: Tempered hardboard is hard, waterproof and cuts cleanly.

The photograph shows an oval table made from one standard sheet of chipboard. The drawing above shows how the hardboard template has been planned.

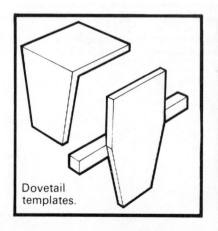

Dovetail templates.

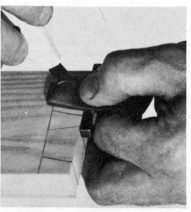

Metal templates are essential when repetitive marking-out must be accurate.
Use for dovetail templates.

Gauges

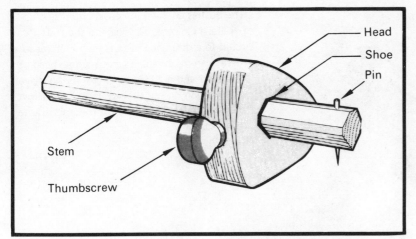

Marking gauge

The beech head is secured on the stem by a plastic thumbscrew — a soft plastic shoe prevents damage to the edge.

Use to mark a line parallel to a face edge, i.e. gauging to width. Hold the head firmly against the face edge to ensure that the steel pin does not wander with the grain.

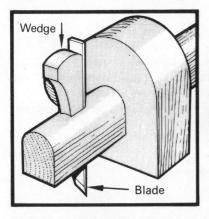

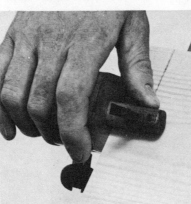

Cutting gauge

The gauge has a cutting blade, secured with a wedge. Use for marking lines across the grain, for example, the shoulder line of a lap or dovetail joint.

Note: The end of the board must be square.

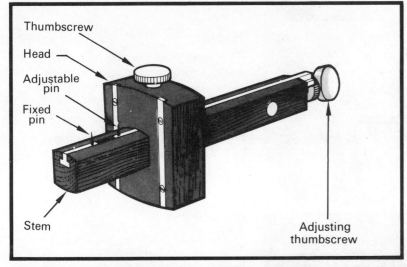

Mortise gauge

The gauge has two pins, one of which is fixed. The other is adjusted by a thumbscrew at the end of the stem and is held in place by the screw which also secures the head. Made from Rosewood and inlaid with brass strips to resist wear.

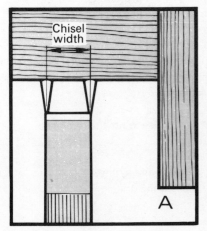

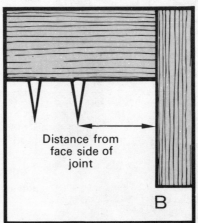

Use for marking out bridle, mortise and tenon and finger joints (see Book 1).
Two settings are necessary :
A the distance between the pins (when marking out a mortise, this must be the chisel width).
B the distance from the face-side or face-edge of a joint.

Cutting Aids
Dowel Jig

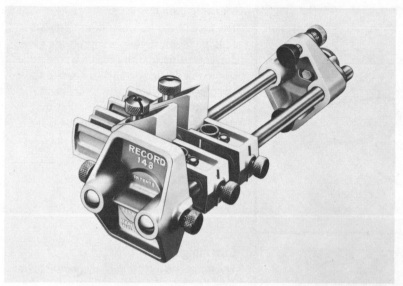

The bushes are held in carriers mounted on parallel slide rods. At one end the rods are fixed to a reference head from which measurements can be taken. The adjustable head at the other end is fitted with two nylon swivel shoes which do not damage wood and allow the jig to be inverted to drill the opposite set of holes.

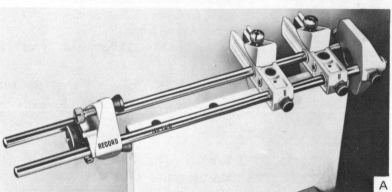

A. Box top or shelf

Hold accurately prepared wood in vice, select and fit rods and bushes.
Secure reference head and position bush carriers at about 75 mm centres.
Set fences to half thickness of timber.
Slide on adjustable head, fix to board and drill both sets of holes.

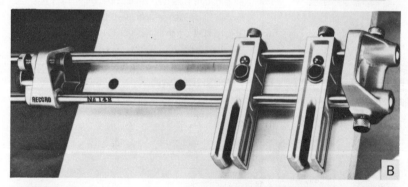

Box side

Remove jig, place in position on box side and drill corresponding holes.

B. Shelf fixing

Square a line across the board to indicate shelf centre. Remove fences, position jig and drill holes.

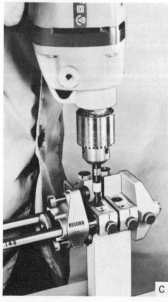

C. Frame joints
The rail

The rail end must be square.
Set bush carriers in position, set fences, fix with the adjustable head and drill holes.

The stile

When cutting corner and tee joints, the jig is held by the jig cramp placed between the bush carriers.

D. When cutting tee joints the reference head is removed.

Depth gauge — use a dowel sleeve or adhesive tape on the drill.

Saws

Those without Backs

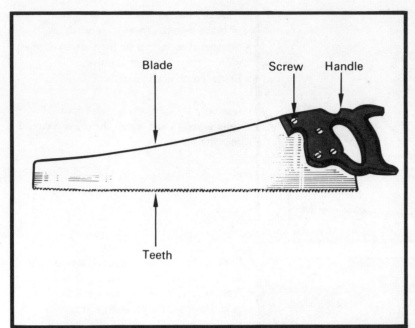

Blade   Screw   Handle

Teeth

All handsaws are similar in appearance but vary in length, teeth size and shape, and the type of handle.

The blade of good quality saws is tapered towards the top edge to prevent the blade from binding.

Use for cutting boards and sheet material.

Saw handles

Wood handles are made of beech with the short grain strengthened by a wood dowel. The handle is screwed through the blade. Plastic handles are moulded into the blade and cannot work loose. The ABS and polypropylene handles are almost unbreakable.

Sawing Techniques

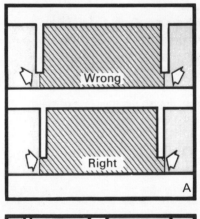

Wrong

Right

A

B

A.   Make saw cuts up to the marked line but on the waste-wood side.
Saw cuts made on the line reduce the size of the wood needed.

B.   When starting a cut, guide the saw with a thumb. Draw the blade upwards several times before cutting on the downward stroke.

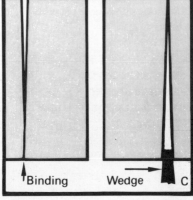

Binding   Wedge   C

D

C.   Saw cuts made down the grain of boards can close up on the saw and cause the blade to 'bind'.
Insert a wedge at the end to open up the cut.

D.   The saw may wander off the line. Correct the fault by bending the handle towards the line on subsequent downward strokes.

Rip Teeth

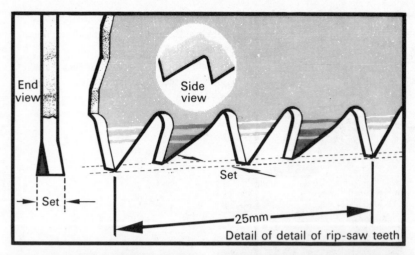

Detail of detail of rip-saw teeth

Rip saws usually have 4 teeth to each 25 mm of blade length. These large teeth are sharpened to form a square cutting edge — each cutting line a small chisel.
Blade length about 650 mm.

Use only for sawing down the grain of solid wood. Used across the grain it would tear the fibres.

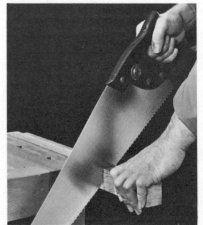

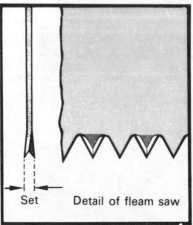

Support long boards between trestles and saw at a fairly steep angle.
Hold shorter boards in the vice. Saw half-way down the length and reverse.

Cross-cut Teeth

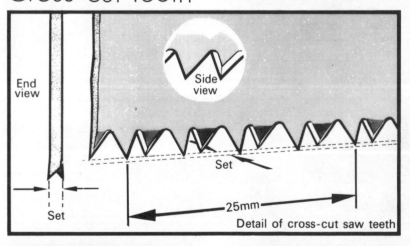

Detail of cross-cut saw teeth

Cross-cut saws have between 6 and 10 teeth to each 25 mm of blade length. The shorter saws with smaller teeth are often called panel saws.
The teeth are sharpened to form a knife-like cutting edge which cuts cleanly across the wood fibres.
Blade length 450 to 600 mm.

Use for cutting across the grain of solid wood and on manufactured boards of all types.

Detail of fleam saw

Saw at a shallow angle to achieve a fine cut and, to prevent 'waste' wood from falling and splitting the grain, support it with your free hand.

Some saws have 'Fleam' teeth. Use where a faster cutting action is needed.
Saws with induction-hardened teeth last a long time but cannot be sharpened.

Those with Backs

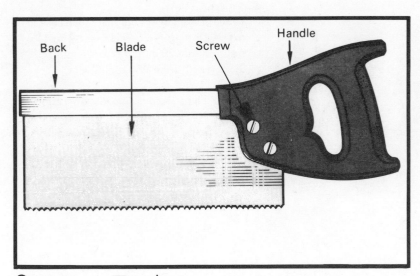

Back   Blade   Screw   Handle

Use saws with a folded steel or brass strengthening edge for detailed work, for example, accurate joint cutting.

All backed saws are similar in appearance but vary in length and teeth size. Handles are made of Beech or plastic.

Sawing Technique

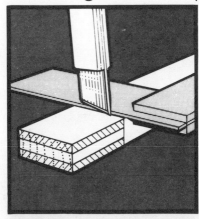
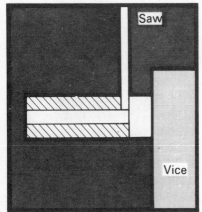

Saw

Vice

Sawing a tenon shoulder.

1. Mark with knife and try square.

2. Hold wood in vice to saw.

3. Cut up to shoulder line on the waste-wood side.

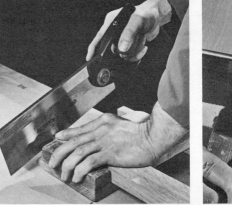

4. Begin cut at far corner of wood. Guide with the thumb and make several light backstrokes.

5. Saw across the whole width of the shoulder and stop at the gauged lines. Keep the saw vertical. Do this by having the forefinger down the side of the handle and keeping the wrist firm.

Tenon Saw

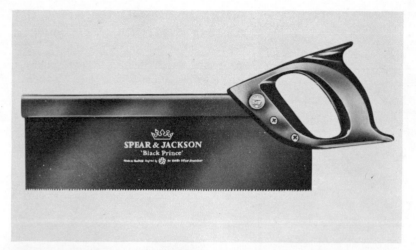

Tenon saw teeth are the same shape as cross-cut saw teeth but are smaller — 12 to 14 teeth to each 25 mm of blade length. Blade length from 250 to 350 mm.

The saw illustrated is coated with Teflon 'S' which gives a smooth cutting action and resists rust. This black surface is available on all hand and backed saws.
Use the saw for general joint work, for example, housings, halvings, bridles, tenons.

When not in use protect the teeth with a plastic guard.

Dovetail Saw

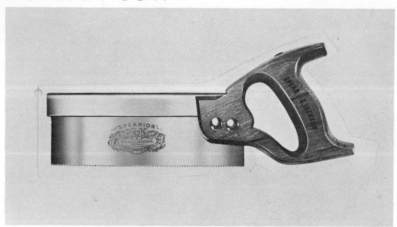

Dovetail saws have 20 teeth to each 25 mm of blade length.
Blade length is 200 mm
Use only for fine work, for example, cutting dovetails, finger joints, shoulders and haunches on small tenons.

Goscut

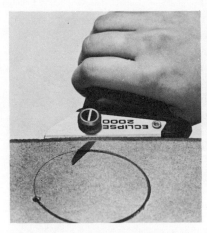

Sheet saws, fitted with a hacksaw-type blade are suitable for cutting sheet metal, plastic laminate and thin plywood.
These jobs can also be done by a new tool — the Goscut.
It has three interchangeable blades.
Red; plastic laminates, plywood and hardboard.
Yellow; sheet metal (steel 19swg, aluminium 16swg).
Blue; cutting circles (a pre-drilled hole is necessary) and curves.
The thick blade has fine teeth which remove a strip of material equal to the blades' thickness.

Variable Teeth Saw

The tapered high-speed steel blade has progressive teeth. The teeth nearest the handle are larger than the teeth near the tip which are ideal for starting cuts.
Alter the handle position for correct balance.
Use on soft and hard plastics, metal and asbestos.

Narrow Blade Saws

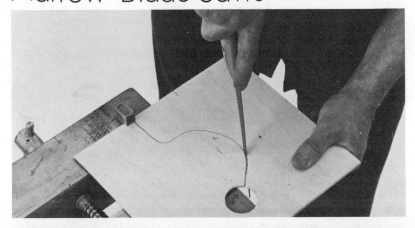

The Stanley trimming knife handle can be fitted with saw blades.
Use the pointed blade for fine work in solid wood and on manufactured board, for example cutting curves and small diameter holes.
Use the square ended blade for sawing metal, plastic and asbestos.

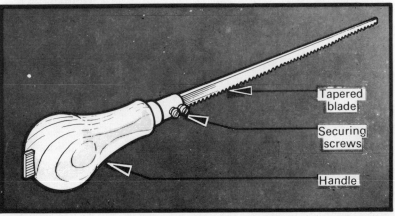

The padsaw
The tapered blade is slotted through the handle and secured with screws. The amount of blade protruding can be adjusted. Use only on wood.

Tapered blade

Securing screws

Handle

Log Saw

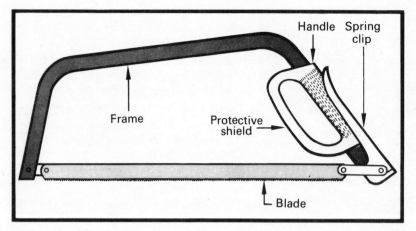

The Teflon 'S' coated blade has induction-hardened teeth, designed to cut on both the forward and backward strokes. It is tensioned with a lever onto a tubular steel frame.
A plastic handgrip protects the knuckles.
Blade lengths 600, 750 and 900 mm
Use for rough sawing logs and sculptural work (see Book 3)

Bow Saw

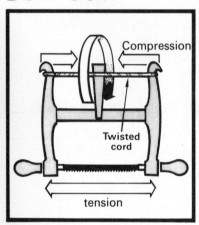

The narrow blade has cross-cut shaped teeth, and is tensioned by twisted cords pulling on the wood frame.
The blade is slotted into brass dowels and held by steel pins.
Blade lengths 200, 250 and 300 mm
Use for sawing curves in thick wood.

Coping Saw

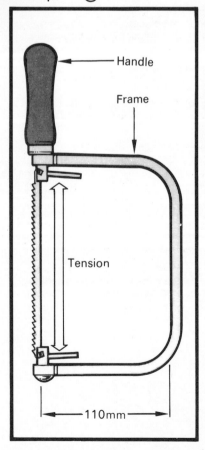

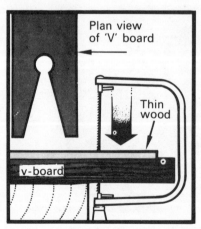

The thin blade cannot be sharpened. It is made cheaply and disposed of when blunt or broken.
It is slotted into each end of the sprung steel frame, which holds the blade in tension.
Fix blade so that teeth cut on the downward stroke.
Blade length 160mm
Use for cutting curves in thin wood.

Hold wood on a V-board fixed to the bench top.

Use for removing waste wood from joints, for example, dovetails.

14

Planes
Wood Jack Plane

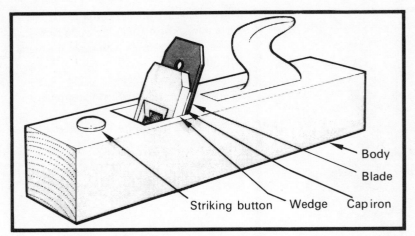

Body
Blade
Striking button Wedge Cap iron

The traditional wood plane is made of beech and is comparitively light to hold. The plane is designed to remove coarse shavings so the cap iron is set about 1·5 mm from the edge of the blade.

The blade and cap iron are screwed together and held in place with a wood wedge. The wedge is released by hitting the striking button with a hammer and simultaneously withdrawing the wedge.

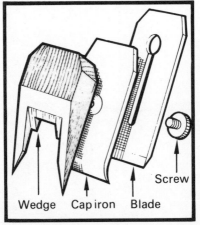

Screw

Wedge Cap iron Blade

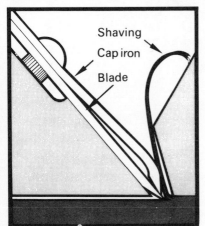

Shaving
Cap iron
Blade

The section shows how the shaving is 'broken' by the cap iron as it comes through the plane mouth.
Ensure that the cap iron fits perfectly. A small gap will cause clogging.

Using a Jack Plane

Planing the edge of a board
At the beginning of the stroke apply pressure at the front of the plane, and at the end transfer pressure to the back.

Planing a surface
Apply pressure evenly. Hold the board on a bench top to give support.

Metal Jack Plane

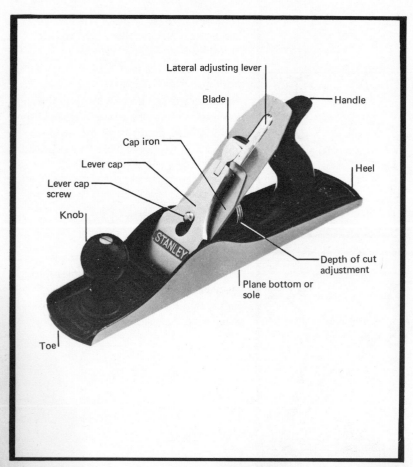

Lateral adjusting lever

Blade

Handle

Cap iron

Lever cap

Lever cap screw

Knob

Heel

Depth of cut adjustment

Plane bottom or sole

Toe

The metal jack plane is heavier to use but has a thinner blade than the wood jack plane. It has the same features as the metal smoothing plane.
1. flat non-wearing sole
2. lever and knob to adjust the amount of cut.
3. adjustable mouth for fine or coarse work

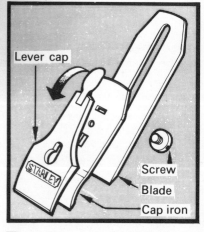

Lever cap

STANLEY

Screw

Blade

Cap iron

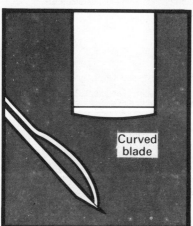

Curved blade

The blade and cap iron are held with a lever cap. Simply flick the lever to release them.

Use the jack plane to smooth rough-sawn wood and to reduce wood quickly to size. To work efficiently the cutting edge of the blade is curved.

Technical Jack Plane

The body of the plane has deep sides, in which a hole is tapped, and cross ribbing to give extra strength.
Fix a side handle to use as a shooting plane.

Metal Smoothing Plane

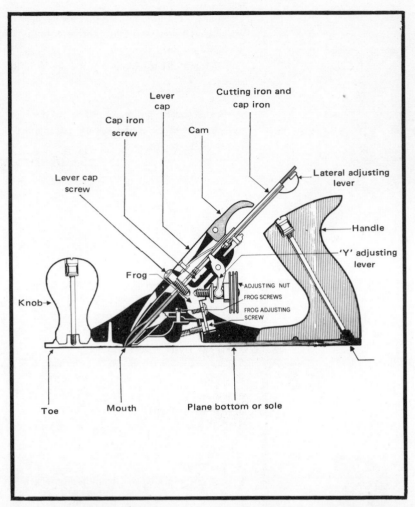

Cap iron screw
Lever cap
Lever cap screw
Cam
Cutting iron and cap iron
Lateral adjusting lever
Handle
'Y' adjusting lever
ADJUSTING NUT
FROG SCREWS
FROG ADJUSTING SCREW
Frog
Knob
Toe
Mouth
Plane bottom or sole

The metal try, jack and smoothing planes have the same basic construction but are different in length and width.

Mouth adjustment

To make the mouth small for fine work, remove the blade assembly and slacken the two frog screws. Close the mouth by turning the frog adjusting screw in a clockwise direction (to open the mouth wider for coarse work turn the screw in an anticlockwise direction). Tighten the frog screws and reassemble.

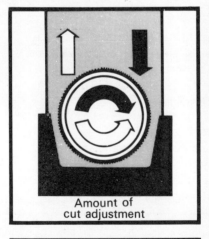

Amount of cut adjustment

Lateral adjustment

Plane inwards from each edge of the board

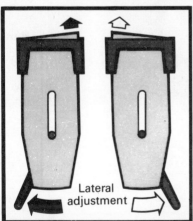

Flat blade corners removed

Cap iron fitted close to cutting edge

Amount of cut adjustment

When too much blade protrudes from the mouth the plane will chatter. This leaves ridges on the wood and can clog the mouth. Correct the setting by turning the adjusting nut which is in front of the handle.
Turn clockwise to produce a coarser cut and anti-clockwise to produce a finer cut.

Lateral adjustment

If the blade protrudes at one side it will dig into the wood surface.
Correct the setting by moving the lateral adjusting lever.

Use the smoothing plane:
1. to produce a fine surface finish
The blade must have a flat cutting edge.
The cap iron must fit well and very close to the cutting edge.
2. to clean up glued joints
3. to square the ends of boards

Metal Try Plane

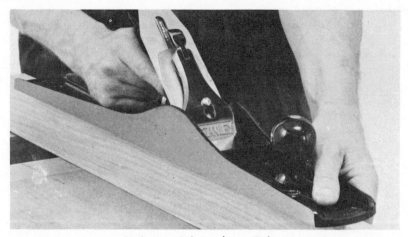

Use the try plane to ensure that long edges are made straight and true , and that large surfaces are flat.
Sharpen and set the blade as for a smoothing plane.

A short smoothing plane tends to follow undulations in the wood but the try plane removes the high spots.

Replaceable Blade Plane

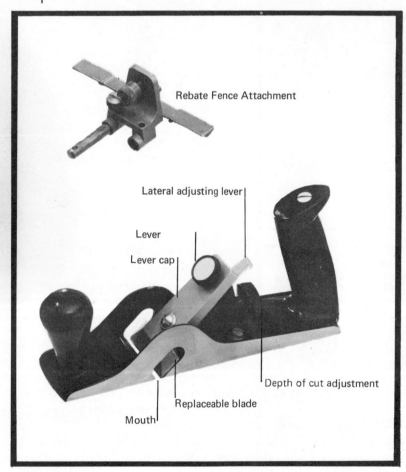

Rebate Fence Attachment

Lateral adjusting lever

Lever

Lever cap

Depth of cut adjustment

Replaceable blade

Mouth

The Stanley RB10F is an adaptable plane which uses narrow disposable blades. These are thrown away when blunted or damaged.
There are three types of blade :—
1. *Curved* — for use on rough surfaces.
2. *Straight* — for finishing surfaces and rebating.
3. *Special* — for trimming laminated plastic sheet.

Adjustment
Lateral and amount of cut adjustments are similar to the standard smoothing plane. The mouth can be altered.

Replacing a blade
Slacken the blade clamping screw and the old blade will drop out of the assembly. Slide in the new blade and re-tighten the blade clamping screw.

Rebate attachment
The blade extends across the full width of the sole.
Fix the fence to either side of the plane to use for rebating.

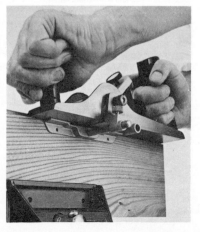

Cabinet Scraper

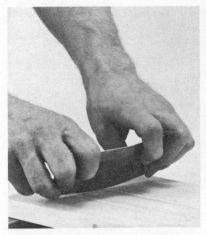

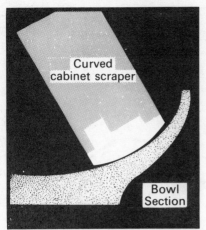

Curved cabinet scraper

Bowl Section

A scraper is made from thin, flexible high-quality steel.
Use to obtain a fine finish on hardwood surfaces which tear when cut with a smoothing plane, for example, twisted grain or irregularities often caused by knots.
Use curved scrapers to smooth out the inside of bowls hollowed with a gouge.

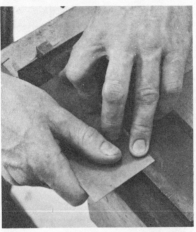

Cutting action
Bend the scraper slightly and use a pushing action. Produce a shaving by sloping the blade until a 'hook' on its edge cuts into the surface.

Producing the cutting edge
1. Draw-file the edge square
2. Ensure accuracy by flatting on an oilstone
3. Hold the blade in a vice and 'draw' the edge over to make a hook. A screwdriver blade can be used.

Scraper Plane

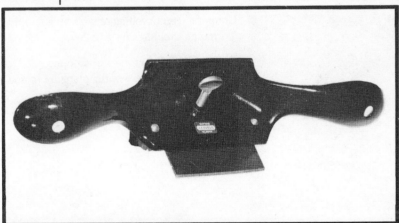

Use the scraper plane for finishing large flat surfaces with awkward grain or veneered surfaces which cannot be planed.
Sharpen the blade at a 45° angle and secure with the clamp.
Use the adjusting thumb screw to bend the blade into a cutting position.

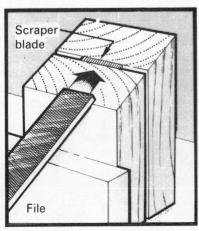

Scraper blade

File

1. The scraper in use.
2. After frequent resharpening refile the angle on the blade holding the blade against a block of wood cut to 45°.

Shoulder Plane

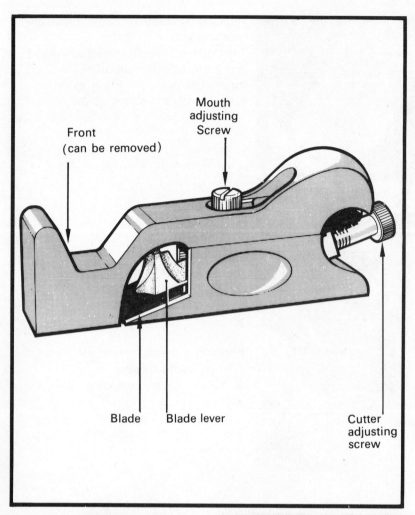

Front
(can be removed)

Mouth
adjusting
Screw

Blade   Blade lever

Cutter
adjusting
screw

The plane illustrated is accurately machined on both sides and is small enough to be used with one hand (140 mm long, blade 20 mm wide). Longer and wider planes are available.

The blade has the sharpening bevel on top and is held by a lever. For fine work move the adjusting slide to reduce the mouth size.

Slacken the lever screw and turn the cutter adjustment to fix the amount to cut.

Common uses: levelling rebates on lap joints. Trimming shoulders of large tenons.

To work into the corners of stopped rebates convert into a chisel plane by removing the front of the plane.

Bull-nose Shoulder Plane

A short plane. Similar to the shoulder plane illustrated above, but with a short nose.

Adjustments can be made to the mouth size and the amount of cut.

The front part can be removed.

Block Plane

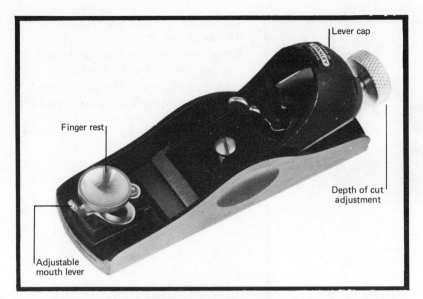

Lever cap

Finger rest

Depth of cut adjustment

Adjustable mouth lever

The block plane blade is normally set at an angle of 20° to the sole.

The low angle plane shown has a blade for planing end grain and trimming plastic laminates.

The blade has the sharpening bevel on top and is held by a lever.

To adjust the amount of cut partly release lever and turn adjusting screw.

To alter the mouth size slacken the finger rest and turn the eccentric plate.

The plane in use
1. Trimming end grain
Keep the plane horizontal but angle the blade so that cutting is easier.

2. Squaring the ends of small sectioned wood held on a shooting board.

3. Trimming plastic laminate
Set the blade finely to prevent chipping.
4. Shaping edges
Light and small enough to use with one hand, for example, making chamfers, bevels and rounds.

Rebate Plane

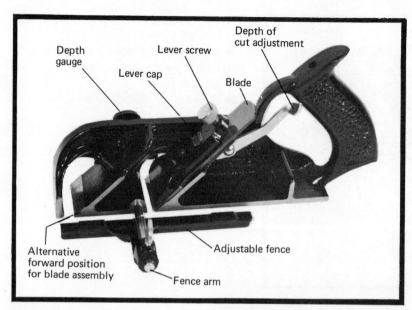

Depth gauge
Lever cap
Lever screw
Depth of cut adjustment
Blade
Alternative forward position for blade assembly
Fence arm
Adjustable fence

The rebate plane is sometimes called a Fillister plane.

For normal use fix the blade in the back position where the amount of cut can be adjusted with a lever. The blade is transferred to the front position for bull-nose work.

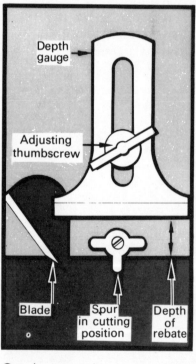

Depth gauge
Adjusting thumbscrew
Blade
Spur in cutting position
Depth of rebate

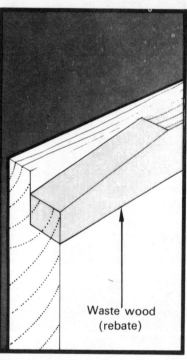

Waste wood (rebate)

Adjust the fence on the fence arm to determine the width of the rebate (maximum cut 38 mm wide).

Adjust the depth gauge to limit the depth of the rebate.

To work cleanly across the grain the wood fibres are cut with a small spur. Use a small screwdriver to rotate the spur into a cutting position.

Start the rebate at the far end of the wood and work back, keeping the fence close to the wood and the plane upright.

Side Rebate Plane

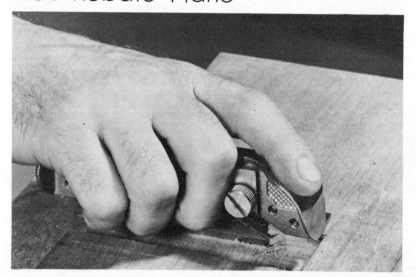

Use the plane to trim the sides of grooves and housings.

There are two blades which can be adjusted separately for amount of cut and which allow for left or right hand working. Set depth gauge to avoid digging into work The photograph shows the end removed to work into the corner of a stopped housing.

Plough Plane

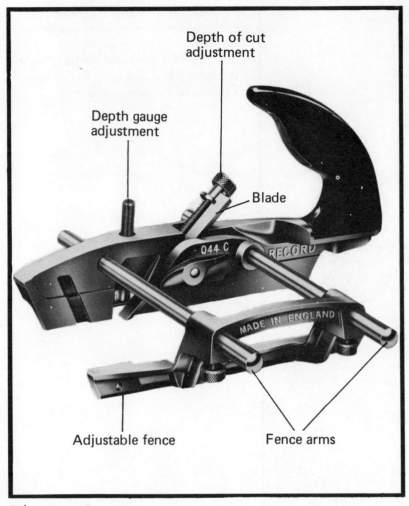

Depth gauge adjustment

Depth of cut adjustment

Blade

044 C   RECORD

MADE IN ENGLAND

Adjustable fence

Fence arms

The plane is used to cut grooves and rebates, parallel to the edge of boards, in which plywood, hardboard or glass panels will fit, for example, cabinet backs and thin sliding doors (see Book 1).
Standard range of blades from 3 mm to 12·5 mm, with 4, 6, 9 and 12 mm blades to match manufactured board thicknesses.

The plane in use
Start the groove at the far end of the wood and work back.
Keep the fence close to the wood and the plane upright.

Plane Settings

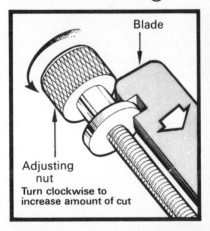

Blade

Adjusting nut
Turn clockwise to increase amount of cut

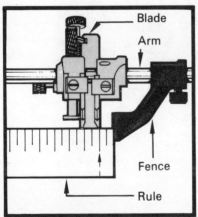

Blade

Arm

Fence

Rule

Before using plough, rebate and combination planes, set and check the following :—
1. **Blade** — the width and amount of cut.
2. **Fence** — select long or short arms. Use a steel rule to set the fence and check on the work itself.

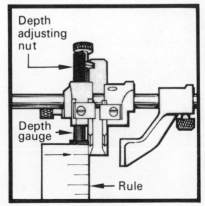

Depth adjusting nut

Depth gauge

Rule

3. **Depth** — use a steel rule to set depth gauge.
4. **Spur** — set in cutting position for working across the grain of solid wood or on manufactured board (N.B. Spurs are not fitted to the plough plane illustrated).

Router Plane

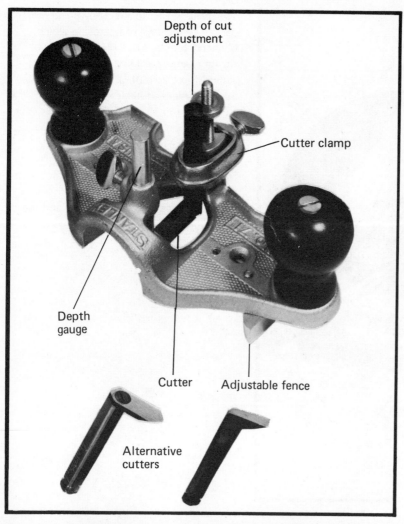

Depth of cut adjustment

Cutter clamp

Depth gauge

Cutter   Adjustable fence

Alternative cutters

A plane designed to level the bottoms of grooves and housings (generally cut across the grain).

There are three alternative cutters. Two are straight (6·5 and 12·5 mm wide) and one is V-shaped for reaching into corners.

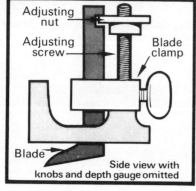

Adjusting nut

Adjusting screw   Blade clamp

Blade   Side view with knobs and depth gauge omitted

Set the depth gauge to prevent the blade from cutting below the required depth.

Increase the amount of cut by releasing the cutter clamp and turning the nut clockwise. Turn the nut anti-clockwise to produce a finer shaving.

Small Router Plane

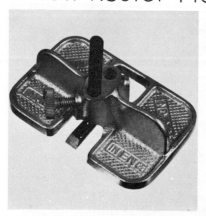

The narrow cutter of this small router plane is fixed with a slotted screw. It has no depth gauge.

Use to level small housings, pushing the plane with fingers and thumbs.

Chisels
Firmer Chisel

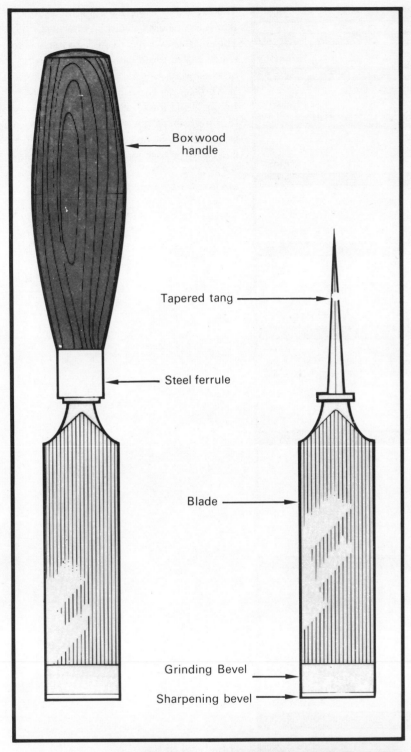

Box wood handle

Tapered tang

Steel ferrule

Blade

Grinding Bevel

Sharpening bevel

A general purpose chisel with a square edge blade strong enough to withstand the chisel being hit with a mallet.
Common sizes (see page 26).

The tapered tang is square in section.

The metal ferrule gives the handle strength where it might otherwise split.
The handle shown is made of close-grained Boxwood.

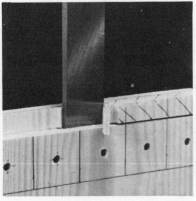

The chisel in use
Use for removing waste from joints such as the housing and the lap joint illustrated.

Bevel-Edge Chisel

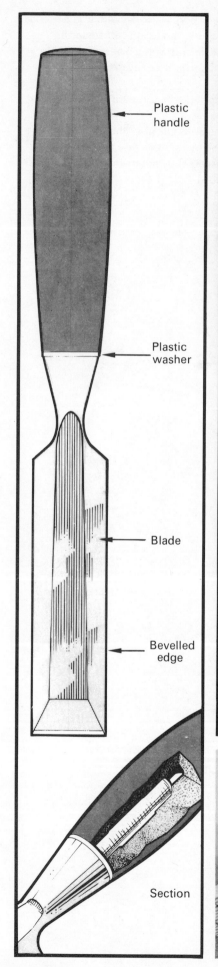

Plastic handle

Plastic washer

Blade

Bevelled edge

Section

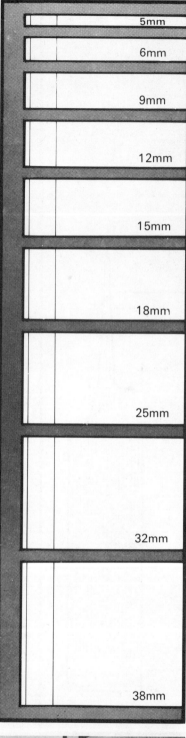

5mm

6mm

9mm

12mm

15mm

18mm

25mm

32mm

38mm

The edges of the blade are ground away so that it can be used to cut into corners.
The chisel shown has an ABS plastic handle which will not split when hit with a mallet or a hammer.
The bolster construction used is ideal to fix blade and the plastic handle together. It is not used with a wooden handle.
Note: narrow bladed chisels are weak and must only be used by hand.

Blade widths from 3 to 38 mm as illustrated.

The chisel in use
Use for cleaning out waste between dovetails.

Mortise Chisels

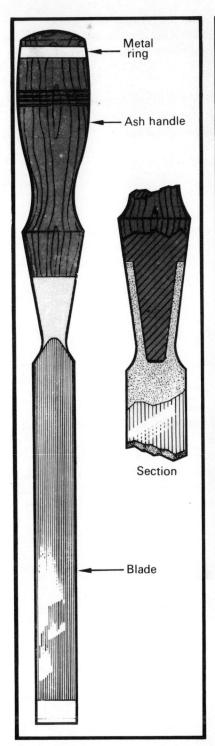

Metal ring

Ash handle

Section

Blade

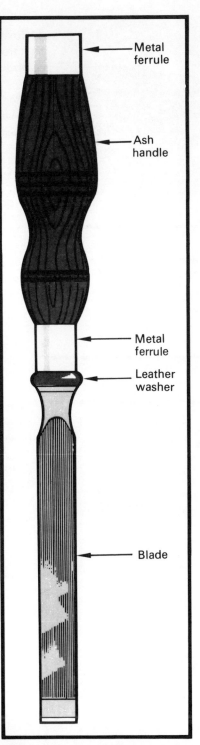

Metal ferrule

Ash handle

Metal ferrule

Leather washer

Blade

Mortise chisels are designed to be hit with a mallet and to lever-out waste wood. The handles shown are made of Ash and are fitted with metal ferrules at the striking end to prevent splitting.

The socket chisel Blade fits over the tapered handle.

The Registered chisel Blade has a tang which fits into the handle in the traditional way (see page 25). A second ferrule prevents splitting and shock is absorbed by a leather washer between the shoulder and the handle.
Blade widths should be 6, 8, 9 and 13 mm but vary slightly.

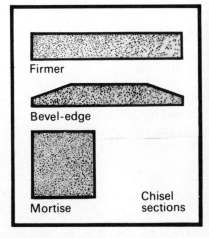

Firmer

Bevel-edge

Mortise

Chisel sections

The blade sections illustrate the comparative thicknesses of the three main types of chisel. The deep mortise chisel permits leverage which would snap a bevel-edge chisel.

The chisel in use
For notes on cutting a mortise (see Book 1).

Boring

Bradawl

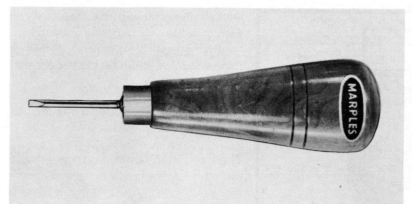

The bradawl has a handle made from Boxwood or Ash. A metal ferrule prevents it from splitting near the shoulder of the blade.

Use to make pilot holes for small screws or large nails and for marking centres in wood to position drills.

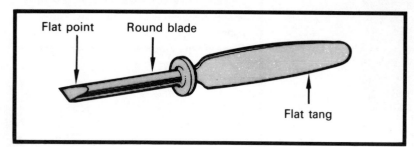

Flat point   Round blade

Flat tang

The cast steel blades are round in section and are sharpened to a flat point.
The tang is flat to prevent it twisting inside the handle.

Hand Drill

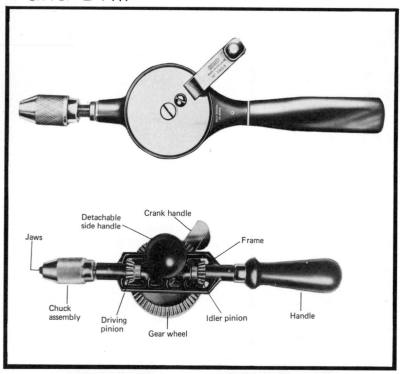

Detachable side handle   Crank handle

Jaws

Frame

Chuck assembly   Driving pinion   Gear wheel   Idler pinion   Handle

The common hand drill has an iron frame, a wood handle and visible gear wheel and pinions.
The modern hand drill has an aluminium casing to which a plastic handle is attached. The enclosed gear wheel and pinions are lubricated with silicon grease and are free from workshop dust.
Both types have a self-centring three-jaw chuck to hold drill shanks up to 8 mm diameter.

The hand drill in use
Use with twist and countersink drills to prepare for screwing.

The bradawl in use
Press the blade into the wood across the grain and twist. If inserted down the grain the wedge action could split the wood.

Joiners Brace

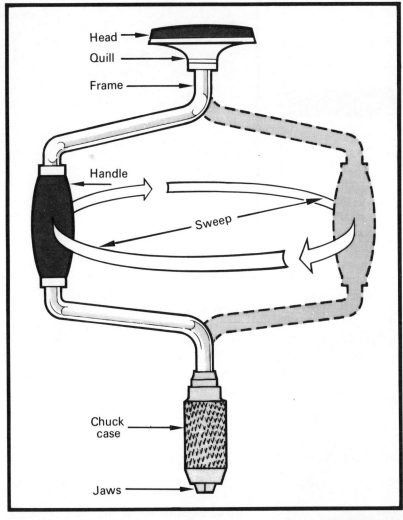

Head
Quill
Frame
Handle
Sweep
Chuck case
Jaws

The illustration shows a plain brace made of steel and fitted with an ABS plastic head and handle. Other braces may look similar but have different design features.

The jaws are either the alligator or the universal type.

The drive can be plain or fitted with a pawl and ratchet (invaluable when working close to a resitricting surface).

The sweep describes the space needed to make one turn of the brace handle. Sizes from 200 to 350 mm.

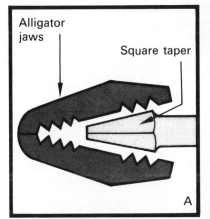

Alligator jaws

Square taper

A

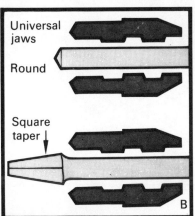

Universal jaws

Round

Square taper

B

A. Alligator jaws for use with square shanked bits which must be carefully positioned in the V-slots.
B. Universal jaws for use with square, taper, morse taper (No. 1) or parallel shank bits up to 13 mm diameter.
C. The brace is normally used as a plain brace but is quickly converted for use in a confined space.

C

Drills

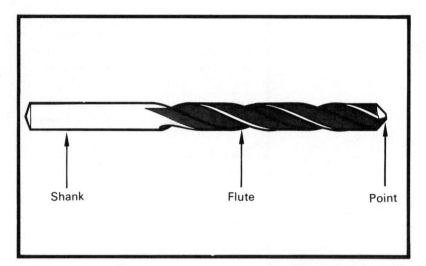

Shank   Flute   Point

The illustration shows a parallel shank twist drill used in three jaw chucks, for example, the hand drill or power unit, to bore small diameter holes.

Centre Bit

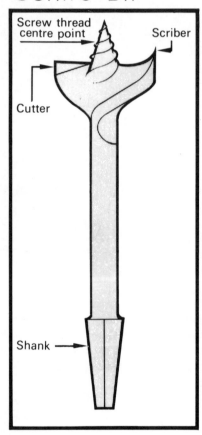

Screw thread centre point   Scriber

Cutter

Shank

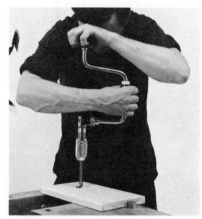

This bit has a threaded centre point which draws the scriber into the work. This severs the wood fibres and the cutter removes the waste.

Use for boring holes up to 50 mm diameter. For vertical boring secure the wood and use a try-square as a guide.

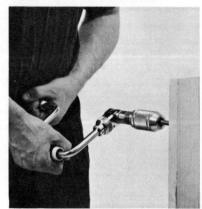

To bore a through hole hold the wood in the vice and hold the brace horizontally. Prevent splitting by cramping waste wood to blind side of hole.

Twist Bit

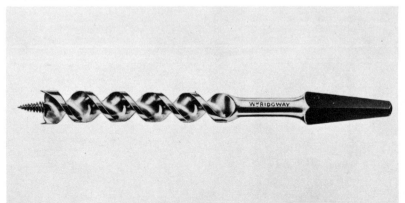

The illustration shows a Jennings type bit which has a cutting action similar to that of the centre bit. The accurately ground twist keeps the bit straight and removes the waste wood when boring deep holes. Use for holes up to 38 mm diameter.

Forstner Bit

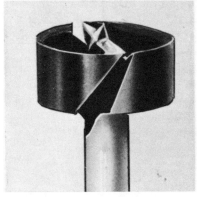

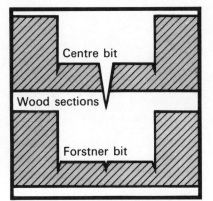

Centre bit

Wood sections

Forstner bit

The Forstner bit has a small centre point and a cutting ring in place of scribers. Cutters inside the ring remove waste wood.

Use to bore a shallow hole in thin wood. The sections show that a centre bit is unsuitable as the screw thread would pierce the back of the wood.

Expansion Bit

The bit is fitted with an adjustable scriber and cutter. Set the slide with a screwdriver and test for accuracy on a piece of waste wood before using on the job.
Use for boring holes (up to 150mm in diameter) in thin wood.

Countersink Bit

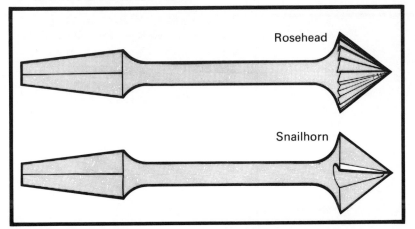

Rosehead

Snailhorn

There are two types of countersink bit:
i Rosehead — for hardwoods.
ii Snailhorn — for softwoods

Dowel Bit

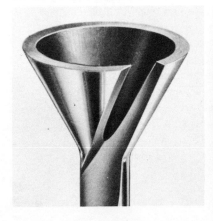

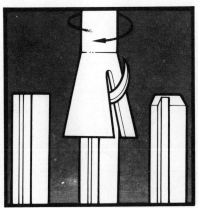

The inside cutter on the cone-shaped head will cut dowel up to 19 mm in diameter.
Use to chamfer the ends of dowel when preparing it for a dowel joint.
An alternative method is to chamfer the dowel on a lathe sander (see page 50).

Driving Tools
Joiners' Mallet

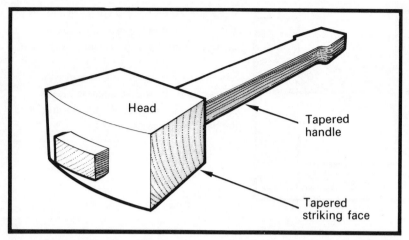

Head

Tapered handle

Tapered striking face

The mallet is made from Beech which is close-grained, hard, smooth and does not easily split. The mallet head and handle fit together without glue or wedges.

The end-grain striking surfaces of the head are slightly tapered. The rectangular mortise through the head is also tapered so that the handle fits tightly into it.

In use the head will not come off — in fact swinging the mallet tightens the fit.

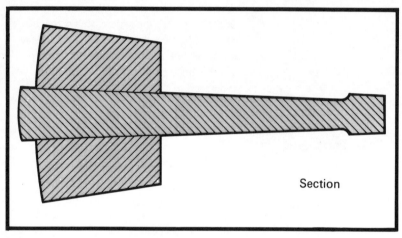

Section

Carvers Mallet

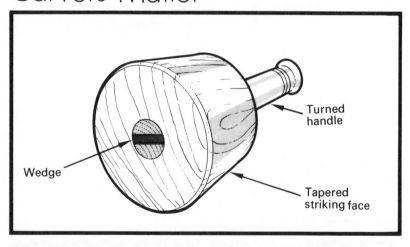

Wedge

Turned handle

Tapered striking face

The best carvers' mallets are made of heavy Lignum Vitae wood — fitted with an Ash handle.

The head is round and tapered with a hole bored through the middle into which the handle is both glued and wedged.

The mallets in use
Hold the joiners' mallet handle near the end. Swing from the elbow to ensure a firm blow on the chisel handle.

The short-handled carvers' mallet allows a wristy action to be used. Both side and end grain are used to form an all-round striking face.

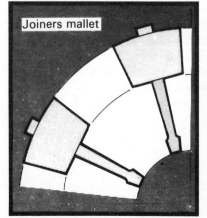

Joiners mallet

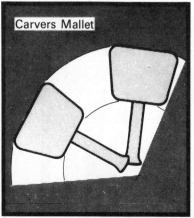

Carvers Mallet

Cross pein Hammer

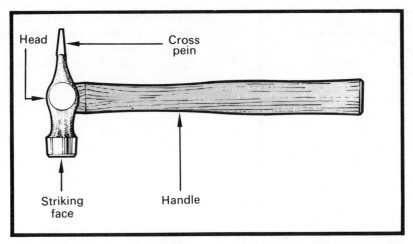

Head — Cross pein

Striking face — Handle

The Warrington hammer head has a polished striking face at one end and a narrow pein at the other. This is used to start a panel pin between finger and thumb.
Never use a cheap hammer. Brittle steel heads will chip and folded steel or poor quality handles will allow the head to fly off on impact.

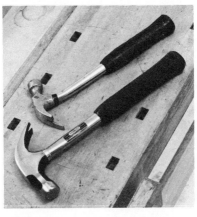

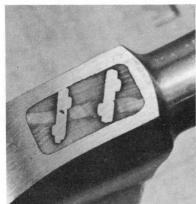

The fit between handle and head is critical. Stanley handles are:
  i. made from pre-shrunk oil-sealed Hickory.
  ii. a hard Hornbeam wedge and two barbed iron wedges are driven in to secure the handle in the eye.

Claw Hammer

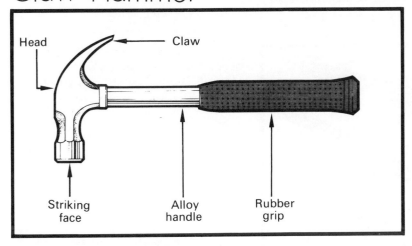

Head — Claw

Striking face — Alloy handle — Rubber grip

Use claw hammers for carpentry and heavy joinery work where large nails are both driven in and withdrawn.

Use the wood handled hammer for regular outdoor work.
(Do not use cheap metal shafted hammers with rubber grips!)

The Hammers in Use

Use the cross pein hammer to drive in a panel pin. Hold the pin between finger and thumb.

To withdraw large nails without damaging the wood surface, lever against waste wood placed under the hammer head.

Soft-faced Hammer

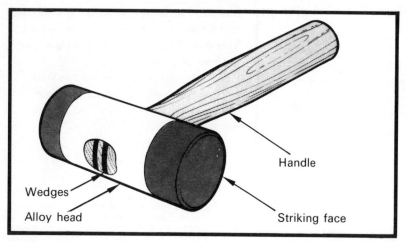

The type shown has two flat faces. One face
(black) is hard but the other (red) is soft and
will not damage softwoods.
The Ash handle is wedged into the aluminium
head.
Damaged heads can be replaced.
Use for fitting joints.

Handle

Wedges

Alloy head

Striking face

Nail Punch

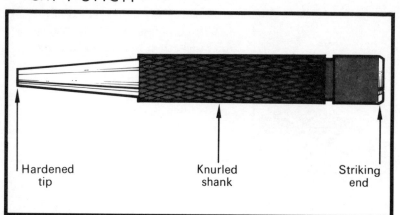

Strike the punch with a hammer to drive
nail heads below the surface of the material.
The surface of the punch is knurled to make
it easy to hold.
The tips are hardened and punches are made
to fit nail heads from 1·5 to 4 mm diameter.

Hardened
tip

Knurled
shank

Striking
end

Pincers

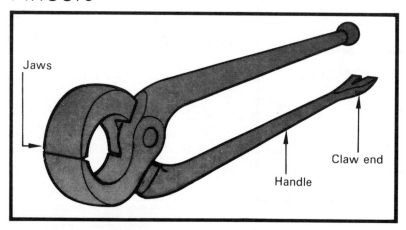

Use pincers to remove small nails from
wood. The rounded jaws help to lever the
nails out. Remove nails in awkward places
with the claw end on one handle.

Jaws

Claw end

Handle

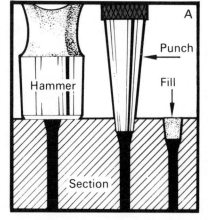

A

Punch

Fill

Hammer

Section

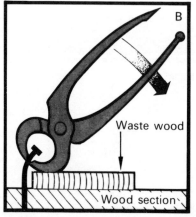

B

Waste wood

Wood section

The tools in use
A. Drive the nail flush
   Punch below surface
   Fill hole and apply finish
B. To withdraw long nails without
damaging the wood surface, lever against
waste wood.

Cabinet Screwdriver

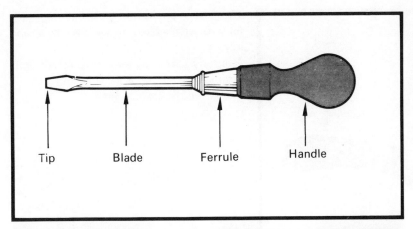

Tip   Blade   Ferrule   Handle

The cabinet screwdriver has a tempered alloy steel blade. It has a wide, flat tang slotted into the wood handle so that a powerful twisting action can be exerted. A metal ferrule prevents the handle from splitting.

A ferrule is not required on splitproof plastic handles.

Blade lengths from 50 to 300 mm — the longest has the widest tip.

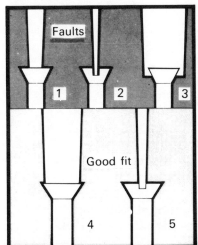

Faults

1   2   3

Good fit

4   5

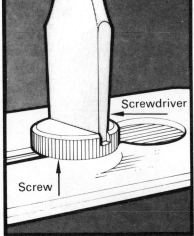

Screwdriver

Screw

Common faults are:
1. Blade too narrow — damage screw.
2. Blade too thin — damage screw and blade.
3. Blade too wide — damage work.

The blade should be:
4. The same width as the head.
5. A firm fit in the slot.
Use a broad screwdriver to remove cap irons from plane blades.

Pozidriv Screwdriver

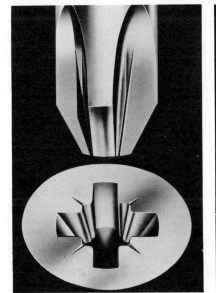

Driver numbers	1	2	3
Screw Numbers	3		
	4		
		5	
		6	
		8	
		10	
			12

The screw head contains a complicated recess into which the distinctive blade is a precise fit. The blade does not 'cam out' and damage the head or the wood surface when force is applied.
The blades are numbered 1, 2 and 3. Check from the table that the correct tip size is being used.
Do not cover the recess with polish or paint.

Spiral Ratchet Screwdriver

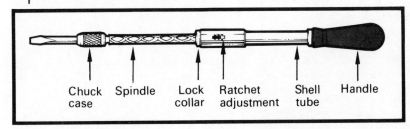

Chuck case   Spindle   Lock collar   Ratchet adjustment   Shell tube   Handle

Use with a pushing action to insert or withdraw large numbers of screws, for example in boatbuilding.
Can be fitted with drill points, flat and Pozidriv tips.

Shaping Tools
Metal Spokeshave

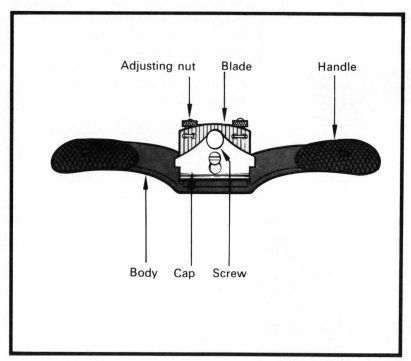

Adjusting nut   Blade   Handle

Body   Cap   Screw

The illustration shows a spokeshave with a fully adjustable blade held in place by a cap iron.

Adjust by slackening the cap iron screw and turning one or both of the adjusting nuts over which the blade is slotted.

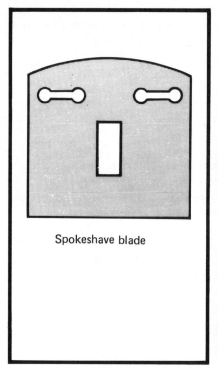

Spokeshave blade

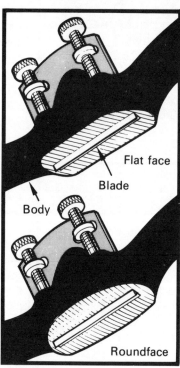

Flat face

Blade

Body

Roundface

The blade is slotted over the adjusting nuts. Fit the blade with the sharpening bevel downwards and secure with the cap iron.

Use a spokeshave with a flat face for smoothing outside (convex) curves.

Use a spokeshave with a round face for smoothing inside (concave) curves

Note: the same straight blade is used in each type.

Spokeshaves in use

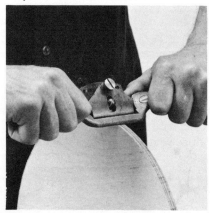

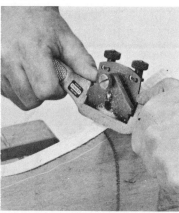

A round-faced tool used to smooth a concave curve on a sculptural form.

A flat-faced tool used on the edge of a plywood stool top.

Outside-ground Gouge

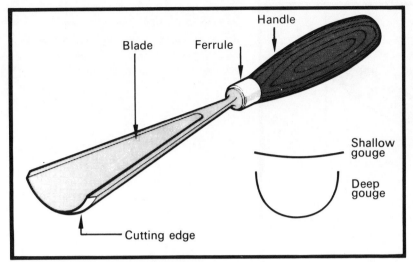

The outside-ground gouge is called a firmer gouge. Blades are made with various degrees of curve — from almost flat to half round. Each blade has a tang which is fitted to the boxwood handle in the same way as the traditional wood chisel. (see page 25). The bevel is ground on a grindstone (see page 40) and sharpened on an oilstone (see page 45).

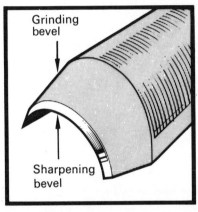

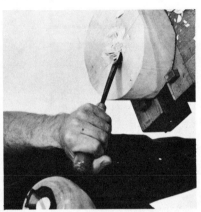

Use the gouge for hollowing out bowls and sculptural work.

Inside-ground Gouge

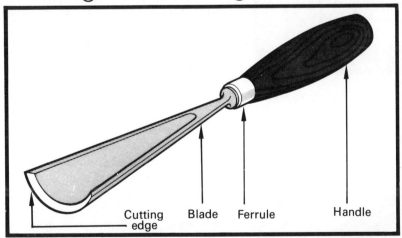

The inside-ground gouge is called a scribing gouge. The bevel is ground on a conical wheel (see page 40) and sharpened with an oilstone slip.

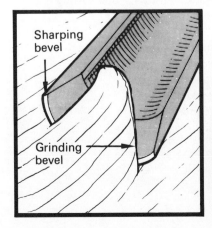

Use the gouge for shaping the outside of bowls, sculptural work and cutting the pockets for pocket screwing (see Book 1).

Filemaster

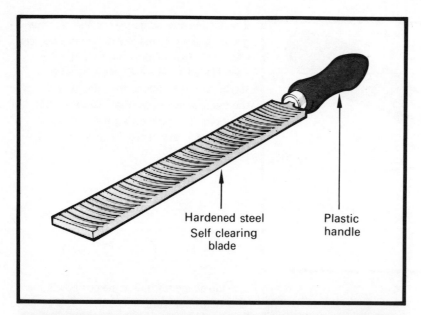

The Aven Filemaster is a general purpose shaping tool which does not clog like the woodworker's rasp or metalworker's file. The fast-cutting teeth keep sharp even when used on metal and plastics.

Hardened steel
Self clearing
blade

Plastic
handle

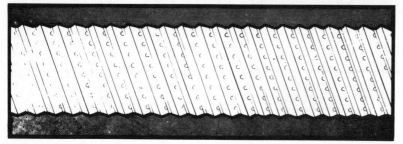

Use the curved teeth for rough shaping especially on wood and soft alloys.

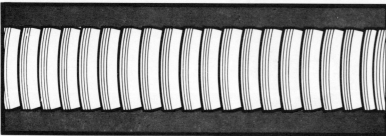

Use the straight teeth for
  i finishing wood and metal surfaces
 ii trimming plastic laminates
iii smoothing synthetic-resin fillers.

Surform Tools

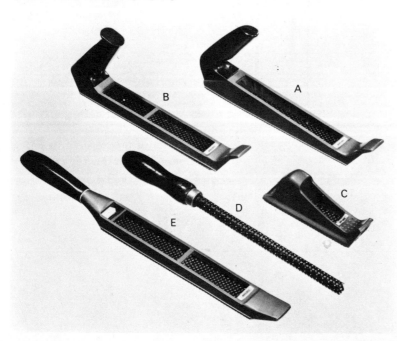

Most 'new' woodworking tools are improved versions of traditional tools. Stanley Surform shaping tools are a product of modern technology-a recent invention.

Each is fitted with a hard non-clogging steel blade with nearly 500 cutting edges on it.

The illustration shows:
A.   Planerfile
B.   Plane
C.   Block plane
D.   Round file
E.   File

Surform Tools

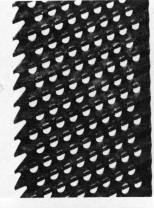

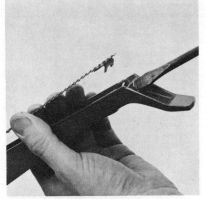

The teeth are shaped and set to cut the material and allow the shavings to pass through the blade without clogging it. The blade cannot be sharpened, set or adjusted. It is replaced when blunt or damaged.

Remove a blade by unscrewing the holding plate at the front of each tool (except the round file).

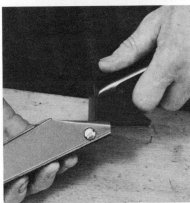

The general purpose 'Planerfile' can be fitted with four types of blade and has two handle positions.

The block plane is used one handed. The photograph shows plastic pipe being trimmed.

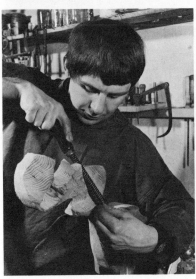

Sculptors in all materials find Surforms invaluable. The photograph shows Michael Smith using a round file. The finished sculpture has been shaped entirely with Surform tools and smoothed with an abrasive.

Manufacturers' recommended blades:

Standard cut

Rapid shaping of softwood, manufactured board, plastic laminates nylon, asbestos, linoleum, rubber, ebonite, leather, cork, glass fibre.

Fine cut

Finishing all the above materials. Also for hardwoods, plywood, aluminium, brass, copper, lead, Perspex and ceramics.

Special cut

Continual use on mild steel, plastic laminates, aluminium, copper, brass and lead.

Maintenance

Grindstones

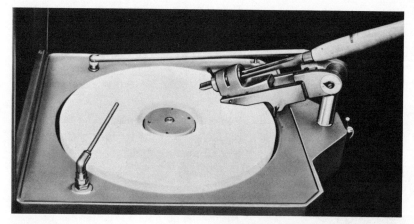

Although some tools have disposable blades most planes and chisels have blades that can be resharpened.
Grindstones are used to give a blade a new grinding angle either when the sharpening angle becomes too steep or when the edge has been chipped.

The photographs show:
  i. A lathe firmer gouge being sharpened on a power driven horizontal artificial grindstone.
  ii. The clamp which holds plane irons up to 75 mm wide. Pre-set the master arm above it to produce the required angle.
  iii. How scribing gouges are ground on a conical wheel projecting from the side of the cabinet.

 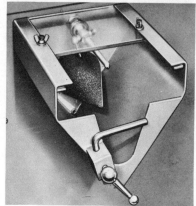

Dry Wheel Grindstone

Dry wheel grindstones are standard equipment in metal workshops. They can be used to regrind blades but the friction heat may burn thin plane blades and narrow chisels.

The blade illustrated has been burnt, i.e., the temper has been 'drawn'. Keep the edge cool by frequently dipping the blade into water.

40

Oilstones

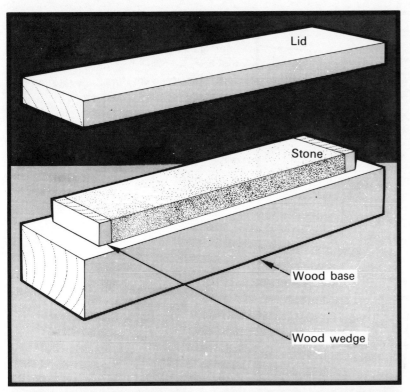

Lid

Stone

Wood base

Wood wedge

Blades are given a razor sharp edge on a fine oil-stone. Artificial oil-stones are a standard size and are made in three grades, coarse, medium and fine.

Protect a stone in a wood block and cover with a lid to keep it free from dust.

Wood wedges placed at each end of the stone and level with it enable the whole oilstone to be used for sharpening.

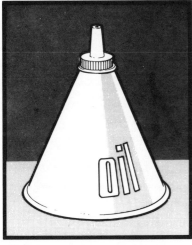

oil

Area worn by chisels

A light machine oil is the ideal lubricant. Heavy or vegetable oils would clog the surface and prevent the stone from cutting
In time, stones become slightly hollow. To re-true the stone, rub it on an old sheet of plate glass sprinkled with Carborundum grit and paraffin.

Oilstone Slips

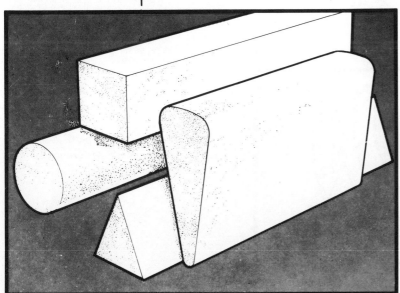

Small artificial oilstones, called slips and files, are made in various shapes and sizes.
Use for sharpening gouges, twist and centre bit scribers and cutters, and the spurs on rebate and combination planes.

Basic Tools

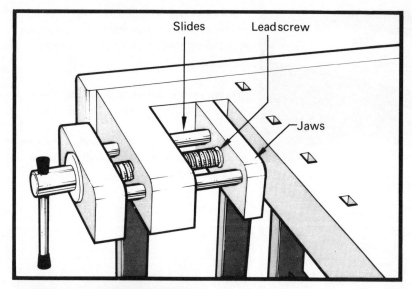

The best tools are expensive and should be protected from rust by laying a sheet of impregnated paper on the bottom of the tool box.

Give tools which are stored in a rack, an occasional rub with an oily rag.

Keep the wood jaws of the vice clean and the slides and lead screw free from dust and shavings. Wipe occasionally with an oily rag.

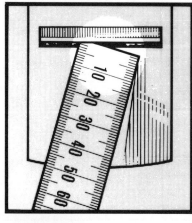

Hammers are 'high impact' tools and are potentially dangerous. Check that the wedges are tight and keep the striking face clean. Remove dirt, grease or glue by rubbing on an abrasive paper. If the handle becomes cracked or worn near the head, renew it.

Important Don'ts

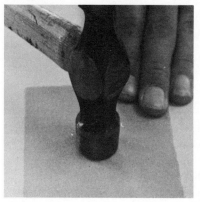

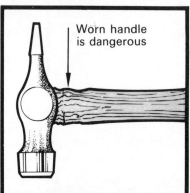

DO NOT use tools for a job for which they are not designed.

DO NOT poke out the shavings blocking a plane mouth.
Remove the blade

DO NOT use a marking knife to apply filler. Use a putty or old table knife.

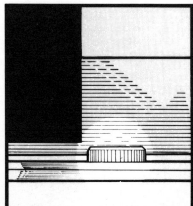

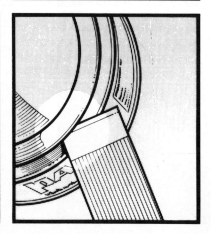

DO NOT use a try square blade to loosen a cap-iron screw. Use a wide-tip screwdriver.

DO NOT open a tin with a chisel. Use an old screwdriver or lever made especially for that purpose.

Saws

Saws not in regular use should occasionally be wiped with an oily rag.

Protect the teeth with a wood or plastic cover strip.

Saws in constant use must be re-sharpened regularly.
Inevitably some teeth wear unevenly or break and the following procedure is then carried out.

Topping
Remove the tops of uneven teeth with a flat file. Make a wood 'Topping clamp' to keep the file flat and square with the saw blade.

Shaping
Remake all teeth the same size and shape using a three-sided saw file. Hold the saw low in the vice and file at right-angles to the blade.

Setting
The amount of set on a saw should produce a cut wide enough to prevent the blade from binding.
Too much 'set' will make sawing difficult and could damage the teeth.
Experts can set the teeth using a hammer.
Alternatively use a plier-type saw set which can be adjusted to control the amount of 'set'.
Alternate teeth are set in the same direction.

Sharpening
Rip saw — produce the square cutting edge by sharpening at 90° to the saw blade.
Cross-cut saw — produce the knife-like cutting edge by sharpening at about 70° to the saw blade.
a) Two or three file strokes will normally be sufficient.
b) Keep the file horizontal.
c) Sharpen alternate teeth in this way.
d) Reverse the saw and repeat.

Rip saw	Cross-cut saw
Handle	Handle
90°	70°

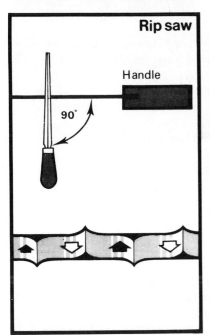

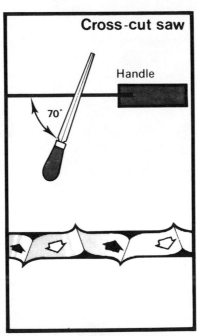

Planes

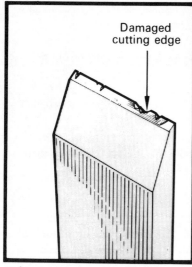

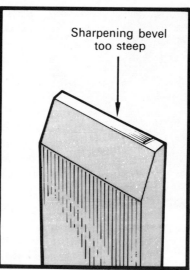

Damaged cutting edge

Sharpening bevel too steep

1. Damaged plane blade
2. Over-sharpened plane blade.
Both must be re-ground at an angle of approximately 25°.

Sharpening a Plane Blade

Sharpen plane blades on a fine oilstone at an angle of about 30°. Use the full length of the stone to prevent excessive wear in the centre.

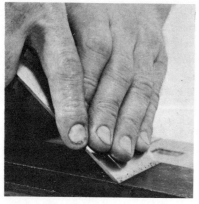

Keep wrists stiff to avoid a rocking motion. This would round the edge and make it blunt.
Sharpening produces a slight burr on the back of the blade. Remove this on the oilstone.
Keep the blade flat.

Cap Iron

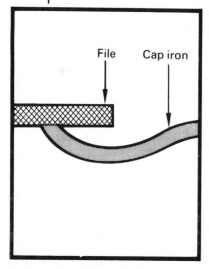

File   Cap iron

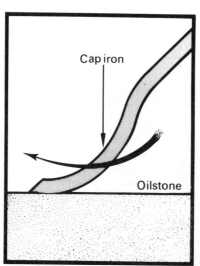

Cap iron

Oilstone

A badly fitting cap iron traps shavings and 'clogs' the plane mouth. Use a smooth file to true the edge.
Smooth off the edge on an oilstone.

Chisels

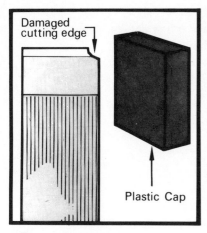

Damaged cutting edge

Plastic Cap

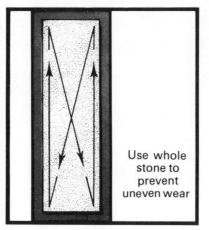

Use whole stone to prevent uneven wear

A damaged chisel blade must be reground. Prevent damage in storage by fitting the blade with a plastic cap.
Sharpen and back off the blade as for plane blade.

Avoid hollowing the stone by sharpening on the edges as well as the middle of the stone.

Gouges

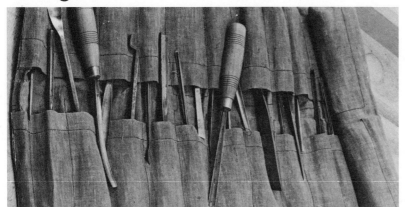

Storage
The delicate cutting edges of the smaller gouges are easily damaged. Store them in racks or in a leather or canvas roll.

Sharpening
Gouge grinding (see page 40)
Sharpen the outside-ground gouge on an oilstone.
Remove the burr with a fine oilstone slip.
Sharpen the inside ground gouge with an oilstone slip.
Remove the burr on an oilstone.

Spokeshaves

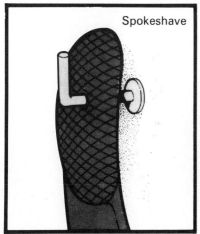

Spokeshave

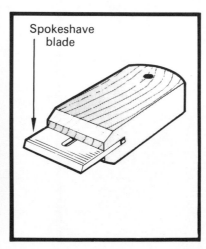

Spokeshave blade

Hang up metal spokeshaves when not in use. Small spokeshave blades slot into a wood block to make sharpening easier. Grind and sharpen as for a plane blade.

Bits

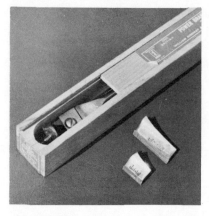

Storage

Centre bits in frequent use are stored in a wood block.
Store twist bits in a rack or canvas roll; Forstner bits and expansive bits in the boxes provided.

Sharpening the cutter

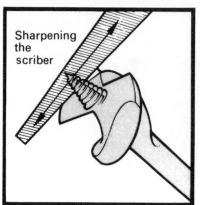

Sharpening the scriber

Sharpening the centre bit

Rest the centre point of the bit on a block of wood and sharpen the cutter with a smooth file.
Remove the burr with a file or oilstone slip (see page 41).
Sharpen the scriber on the inside only — **do NOT touch the outside surface.**

Screwdrivers

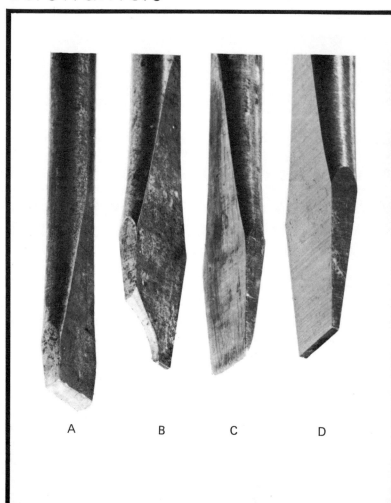

A   B   C   D

Screwdriver A has been reground frequently. The tip is too thick for the screw slot.
Screwdriver B has been misused and is badly chipped.
Screwdriver C has been in constant use and the tip is rounded. This common fault results in the screwdriver slipping out of the slot and damaging the surface of the work.
All these screwdrivers must be reground.

Screwdriver D is cross-ground to produce a squared tip which will fit a screw slot.

Machine Tools
General Safety

Most machine tools can cause serious injury if they are not used correctly. Never use a machine tool until you have been shown how to operate it.

1. Check position of the ON-OFF switch and power isolator.
2. Check the cable. If damaged, do not use.
3. Check that the plug is firmly in the power socket.
4. Fire extinguisher and first-aid kit must be available.
5. One person only to operate the tool at any one time.
6. Do not interfere with the operator.
7. Do not tamper with the machine.
8. Before adjusting the tool, isolate power.
9. Wear protective clothing.

Wiring a Plug

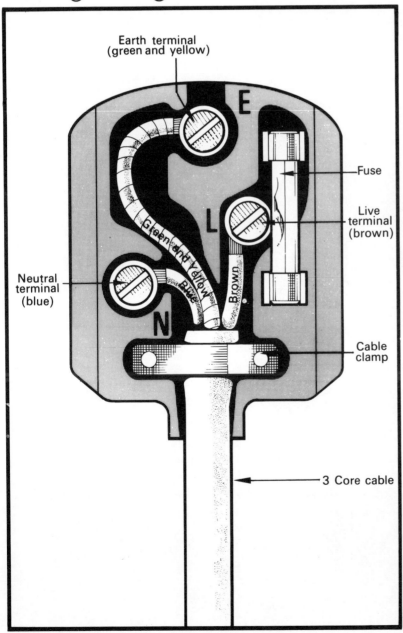

Earth terminal (green and yellow)

E

Fuse

L

Live terminal (brown)

Neutral terminal (blue)

N

Cable clamp

3 Core cable

Important: connect the wires to the correct terminals as shown in the diagram.

Follow this procedure:

1. Connect the **earth wire (green and yellow)** to terminal E.
2. Connect the **live wire (brown)** to terminal L.
3. Connect the **neutral wire (blue)** to terminal N.
4. Secure the power cable with the clamp.
5. Replace top of plug.

A mistake in the wiring could cause the tool to become live!

Handtools with nylon-filled plastic bodies (double insulated) are fitted with a two core cable. Wire as recommended omitting the earth wire (green and yellow).

Protective Clothing

All benchwork
Sanding
Polishing
Painting

Protective clothing will be an apron, smock or overall. These are temporary coverings to protect everyday clothes. If wearing old clothes, do not wear a tie or belt.

Eye Protection

Lathe
Circular saw
Jigsaw
Dry wheel grindstone

The lathe, circular saw and grindstone, revolve quickly towards the operator whose eyes can easily be damaged by flying particles. The portable jigsaw (see page 56). cuts upwards towards the operator.
Always wear clear, ventilated goggles or protective glasses.

Protection from Dust

Lathe
Circular saw
Bandsaw
Jigsaw
Sanding

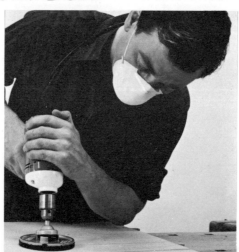

Fine wood dust irritates the mouth and throat.
Operators who suffer with bronchial trouble should wear a mask.
The hygienic paper mask shown, efficiently filters the air and is comfortable to wear.
Do NOT share a mask with another person.

Pillar Drill

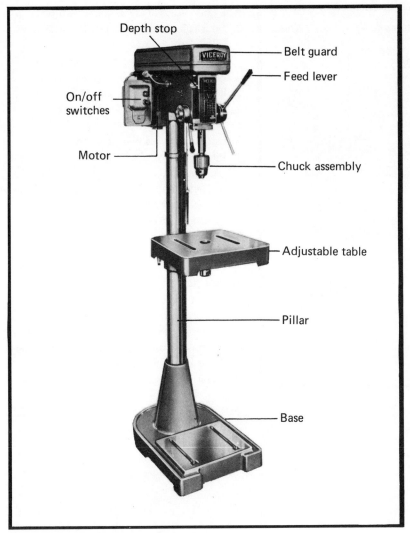

Depth stop

Belt guard

Feed lever

On/off switches

Motor

Chuck assembly

Adjustable table

Pillar

Base

The pillar drill illustrated has the following features :

1. Four spindle speeds (420, 670, 1250, 2150 rpm)
   A lever releases tension on the driving belt to make speed change easier.
2. A metal guard protects the pulleys. If this is not closed, a microswitch isolates the power.
3. Clear on (green) and off (red) switches with emergency stop foot-operated switch.
4. Built in operator's light for better visibility.
5. Drilling capacity 19mm. The chuck can be covered by a plastic guard.
6. A mortising attachment is available.

Safety notes:
(a) Select correct speed for material and drill size.
(b) Ensure drill is tight in chuck. Remove key.
(c) Clamp work down when possible.

Boring Tools

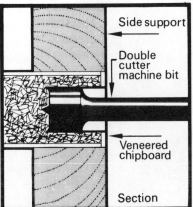

Side support

Double cutter machine bit

Veneered chipboard

Section

Flatbit
Designed for use with power tools.
The spur, centre point and cutter are cut from flat steel and are sharpened with a smooth file.

Double cutter
A precision drill with two cutters — ideal for drilling manufactured boards.
Note: Support chipboard to prevent the fibres 'breaking out'.

Use when fitting KD nylon inserts (see Book 1).

Wood Lathe

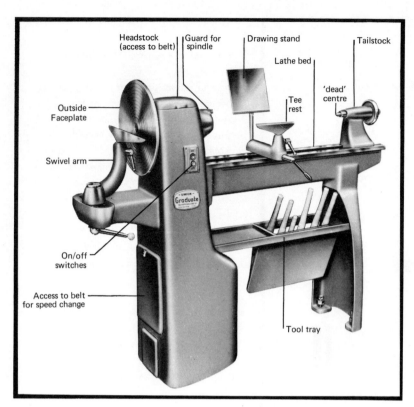

Headstock (access to belt) • Guard for spindle • Drawing stand • Lathe bed • Tailstock • Tee rest • 'dead' centre • Outside Faceplate • Swivel arm • On/off switches • Access to belt for speed change • Tool tray

The lathe illustrated has these features:

1. Four spindle speeds: (425 790 1330 and 2250 rpm)
   A lever releases tension on the driving belt to make speed change easier.
2. The pulleys are enclosed. If the covers are left open, a microswitch on both, isolates the power.
3. On/off switches near operator.
4. Pilot light (not shown).
5. Capacity
   (a) between centres 750 1050 or 1350 mm
   (b) on outer faceplate 300mm diameter
   (c) on outer faceplate 480mm diameter.
6. Accurately machined bed supports sliding tool rest and tailstock.

Safety notes:

(a) Select correct speed for work to be turned
(b) Ensure work is secure to faceplate or between centres
(c) Spin work by hand to ensure that it clears lathe bed and tool rest
(d) Wear protective clothing and goggles.

Attachments

The sanding table is fitted into the outer tool-rest arm and can be tilted to an angle of 45°.
To work accurately, hold wood against sliding fence. Glue abrasive discs (up to 300mm diameter) to a plywood backing and screw on to the outer faceplate.

Safety notes:

(a) Use only to centre of sanding disc (arrowed).
(b) Wear protective mask.

The curved tool rest is used for keeping close to internal surfaces, eg. bowls.

Circular Saw

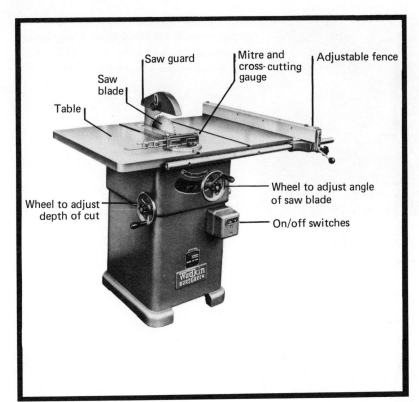

Saw guard

Mitre and cross-cutting gauge

Adjustable fence

Saw blade

Table

Wheel to adjust angle of saw blade

Wheel to adjust depth of cut

On/off switches

The saw illustrated has these features :
1. Saw blade, 250mm dia.
2. Maximum depth of cut, 80mm.
3. Maximum distance from blade to side of table, 650mm.
4. Maximum distance from blade to front of table, 330mm.
5. Saw blade can be tilted to an angle of 45°.
6. Saw guard adjustable on riving knife.
7. On/off switches near to operator.

Safety

(a) Adjust saw guard to suit thickness of wood being cut.
(b) Lock blade adjusting handwheels.
(c) Push narrow material through with a push stick as illustrated.
(d) Protect eyes.

Circular Saw Settings

Handwheels
A for adjusting height of blade
B for changing angle of cut.

Ripping fence has both rapid and micro-adjustment. Read off distance from blade to fence on scale inserted in the guide bar. Lever locks fence at both ends of table.

Ripping and Cross Cutting

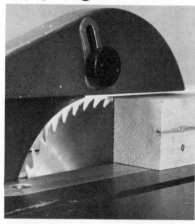

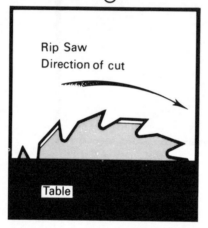

Rip saw blade teeth are designed to saw wood quickly along the grain only.
Check position of fence. Use a push-stick.

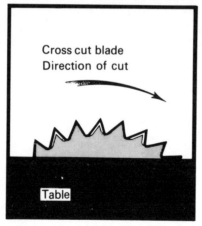

Cross-cut saw blade has smaller teeth sharpened at an angle to cut the wood fibres across the grain.
Use also for manufactured board.
Check the mitre gauge. For repetition cross-cutting set the length gauge.

Grooving

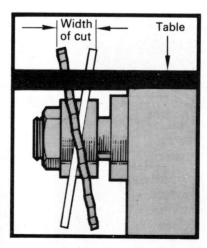

Grooving
The photograph shows twin combination saw blades (rip and cross-cut teeth) being used to cut a 20mm wide groove across the grain.

The wobble saw
This is a thick blade which is held on the saw spindle between wedge-shaped collars. The width of the groove cut depends on the amount of saw wobble. This is adjusted by altering the relationship of the blade to the collars.
Use along the grain.

Bandsaw

The saw illustrated has these features :
1. Saw pulleys (1000rpm) are enclosed.
2. Top pulley adjustment by handwheel and screw.
3. Blade tension and tracking adjustment by handwheel (at rear of machine.)
4. Fence with micro-adjustment and locking lever. Use at either side of blade.
5. Foot operated brake.
6. Table tilts to an angle of 45°.
7. Brush keeps pulley rim free from dust.
8. Maximum throat 490mm.
9. Maximum depth under saw guide 330mm.
10. On/off switches near the operator.

Labels on image: Doors cover pulleys; On/off switches; Adjustable fence; Saw tensioning wheel; Max. depth; Throat; Depth of cut and saw tracking adjustments; Table; Lower saw pulley driven by motor; Foot-operated brake

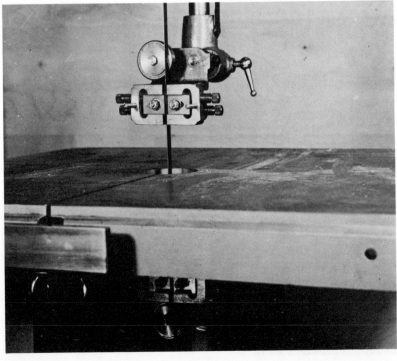

Safety notes:
(a) Check blade tension and tracking
(b) Ensure that top saw guide is clear of work to be cut
(c) Check saw guides

The saw guides are positioned above and below the saw table. They support the blade at either side of the cutting position and must be accurately set. The type shown has a revolving wheel to support the back edge of the blade and adjustable side rollers to give side support and prevent twisting.

Portable Electrical Tools

Power Unit

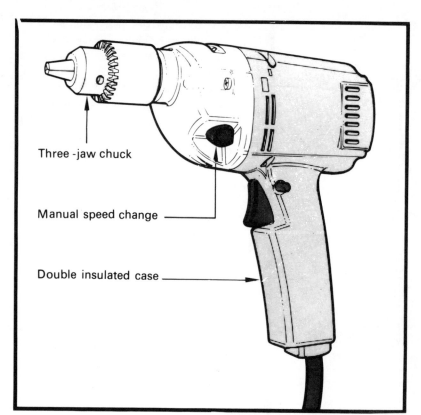

Three-jaw chuck

Manual speed change

Double insulated case

This is commonly known as an electric drill. Its main use is to drill holes in a whole range of materials including wood, metal and masonry.

To do these jobs safely both indoors and out the most suitable unit would have:—

1. A double insulated case identified by this symbol ▣
2. A three-jaw chuck to hold drill shanks up to 12mm dia.
3. Two or more speeds
4. Automatic cut-out to prevent overloading.

Approximate drilling capacities:

Steel	12mm diameter
Masonry	19mm
Hardwood	32mm
Softwood	38mm

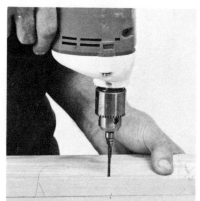

The unit is best used for repetition work where a large number of similar holes must be drilled. In boatbuilding, for example, the unit fitted with a Stanley Screwsink will prepare pilot clearance holes and counter-sinks in one operation.

Larger holes can be bored with a flatbit (see page 49) or the saw-tooth centre bit which has a maximum diameter of 75mm.

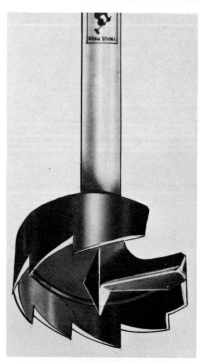

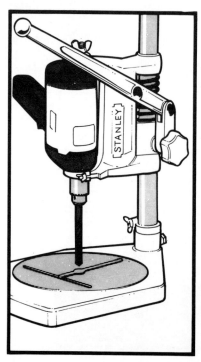

The unit is not always hand held. Screwed into a drill stand it becomes an effective bench-top pillar drill.

The 'electric drill' is the power unit for a wide range of attachments including a circular saw, jig-saw, lathe, sanders, paint spray and hedgecutters.

Typical speeds to power the full range of attachments are:

690 rpm drilling masonry, glass and hard steel.
900 rpm woodturning, drilling hardwoods and mild steel.
2200 rpm drilling softwoods, plywood and for polishing.
3100 rpm circular saws, jig-saws and other attachments.

Sanding Machines

The 125mm disc sander attachment has either a flexible rubber or a soft foam base.
Use especially for coarse sanding and take care to avoid 'scoring' the work.

Remove the abrasive disc and fit a lambswool cover for polishing large surfaces.

Orbital Sander

Motor casing

Handle

Locking button

Trigger switch

Abrasive sheet clip rod

Rubber pad

Abrasive sheet

Use with fine abrasive sheets to produce a wood surface suitable for 'finishing'. It must not be used with coarse grits to remove polishes etc. Use flat, without applying much pressure, and avoid scratches by working along the grain.

Contact area 200 x 100 mm
Speed 5000 rpm

Belt Sander

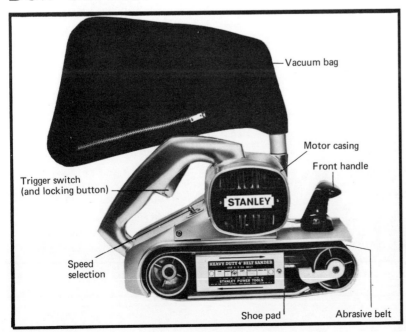

Vacuum bag

Motor casing

Front handle

Trigger switch
(and locking button)

STANLEY

Speed selection

Shoe pad

Abrasive belt

HEAVY DUTY 4" BELT SANDER

The 100mm wide abrasive belt is designed for heavy-duty use on this two-speed machine.
A vacuum removes most of the dust particles.

Abrasives for machine use
Aluminium Oxide
Silicon Carbide
Tungsten Carbide

Jig saws

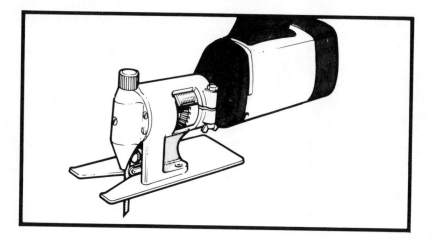

The jig-saw attachment can be used to cut a variety of sheet materials. Select the correct blade for cutting each material; wood, plastic and metal. Approximate capacity in softwood is 50mm.

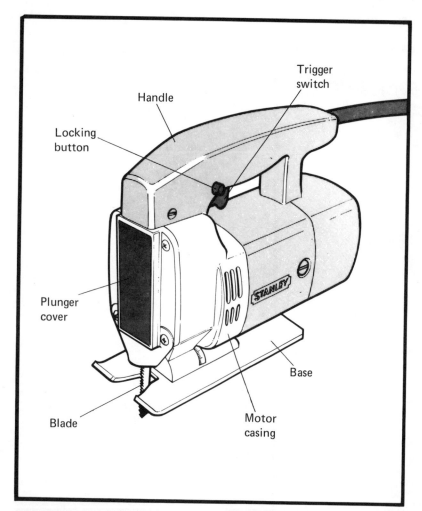

Trigger switch

Handle

Locking button

Plunger cover

Blade

Motor casing

Base

A purpose-built double insulated saw which will make 3000 strokes per minute. The base can be fixed in two positions (one for plunge cutting) and will tilt to 45°.

All jig-saws cut on the upward stroke. Cramp the work firmly face downwards. This lessens the vibrations and reduces the possibility of chipping the surface.

Begin internal cuts through a pre-bored hole or in relatively thin materials, by plunge cutting (as illustrated).

For cutting sculptural shapes it is quicker and more accurate than the bow saw.
It can be used on large sheets which cannot be handled on a band saw or circular saw.

Router

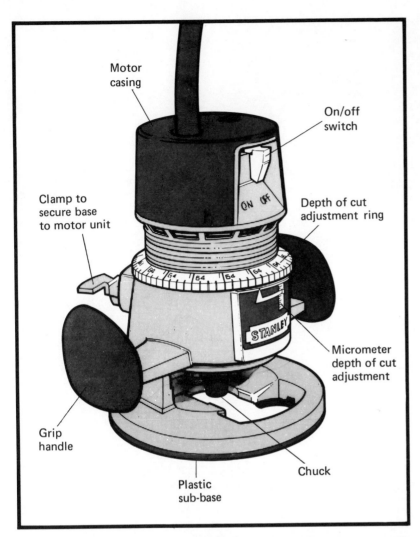

Motor casing

On/off switch

Clamp to secure base to motor unit

Depth of cut adjustment ring

Micrometer depth of cut adjustment

Grip handle

Chuck

Plastic sub-base

The portable router will groove, mould, rebate and trim wood, aluminium and plastic with speed and accuracy. There is a wide variety of tungsten carbide cutters which revolve at more than 20,000 rpm cutting quickly and leaving a good finish.

It is fitted with a fence for straight or circular cuts and can be adjusted for depth of cut to an accuracy of 0·1 mm.

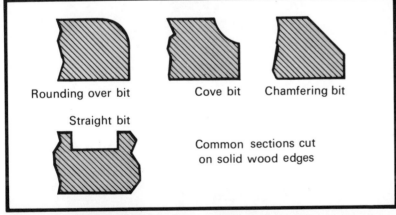

Rounding over bit

Cove bit

Chamfering bit

Straight bit

Common sections cut on solid wood edges

Cutters

These are made to produce a variety of sections and for incised lettering, inlaying and hinge fitting. Grinding wheels are also available.

Grooving manufactured board using a straight edge cramped in position as the guide.

Detail of edge chamfering on a table top.